New Directions for
Teaching and Learning

Marilla D. Svinicki
EDITOR-IN-CHIEF

R. Eugene Rice
CONSULTING EDITOR

Enhancing Learning with Laptops in the Classroom

Linda B. Nilson
Barbara E. Weaver

EDITORS

Number 101 • Spring 2005
Jossey-Bass
San Francisco

ENHANCING LEARNING WITH LAPTOPS IN THE CLASSROOM
Linda B. Nilson, Barbara E. Weaver (eds.)
New Directions for Teaching and Learning, no. 101
Marilla D. Svinicki, Editor-in-Chief
R. Eugene Rice, Consulting Editor

Microfilm copies of issues and articles are available in 16mm and 35mm, as well as microfiche in 105mm, through University Microfilms Inc., 300 North Zeeb Road, Ann Arbor, Michigan 48106-1346.

NEW DIRECTIONS FOR TEACHING AND LEARNING (ISSN 0271-0633, electronic ISSN 1536-0768) is part of The Jossey-Bass Higher and Adult Education Series and is published quarterly by Wiley Subscription Services, Inc., A Wiley Company, at Jossey-Bass, 989 Market Street, San Francisco, California 94103-1741. Periodicals postage paid at San Francisco, California, and at additional mailing offices. POSTMASTER: Send address changes to New Directions for Teaching and Learning, Jossey-Bass, 989 Market Street, San Francisco, California 94103-1741.

New Directions for Teaching and Learning is indexed in College Student Personnel Abstracts, Contents Pages in Education, and Current Index to Journals in Education (ERIC).

SUBSCRIPTIONS cost $80 for individuals and $170 for institutions, agencies, and libraries. Prices subject to change. See order form at end of book.

EDITORIAL CORRESPONDENCE should be sent to the editor-in-chief, Marilla D. Svinicki, Department of Educational Psychology, University of Texas at Austin, One University Station, D5800, Austin, TX 78712.

www.josseybass.com

Contents

FROM THE SERIES EDITOR

About This Publication. Since 1980, *New Directions for Teaching and Learning (NDTL)* has brought a unique blend of theory, research, and practice to leaders in postsecondary education. *NDTL* sourcebooks strive not only for solid substance but also for timeliness, compactness, and accessibility.

The series has four goals: to inform readers about current and future directions in teaching and learning in postsecondary education, to illuminate the context that shapes these new directions, to illustrate these new directions through examples from real settings, and to propose ways in which these new directions can be incorporated into still other settings.

This publication reflects the view that teaching deserves respect as a high form of scholarship. We believe that significant scholarship is conducted not only by researchers who report results of empirical investigations but also by practitioners who share disciplined reflections about teaching. Contributors to *NDTL* approach questions of teaching and learning as seriously as they approach substantive questions in their own disciplines, and they deal not only with pedagogical issues but also with the intellectual and social context in which these issues arise. Authors deal on the one hand with theory and research and on the other with practice, and they translate from research and theory to practice and back again.

About This Volume. This issue of *NDTL* addresses a new movement in higher education to make computing a more integral part of the everyday classroom. Often referred to as laptop initiatives, programs of this sort regularly bring student computer use into the everyday classroom. This issue discusses how one institution and faculty from several disciplines made the transition to more integrated use of computers in classes of all types.

Marilla D. Svinicki
Editor-in-Chief

MARILLA D. SVINICKI is associate professor of educational psychology at the University of Texas at Austin.

EDITORS' NOTES

This volume of *New Directions in Teaching and Learning* is the first major publication on teaching with laptops in the classroom. Its primary purpose is to show that university instructors can and do make pedagogically productive and novel use of laptops in the classroom. As the chapters illustrate, laptops indeed offer rich new opportunities to make classes more student-active, thereby enhancing student engagement and learning. Moreover, these benefits can accrue without compromising the quality of student-instructor interaction or increasing the student workload.

This volume also has a timely secondary purpose: to advise institutional leaders on how to make a laptop mandate successful at their university. Recently, some such mandates have failed or have been canceled or scaled back. It seems that, without help, faculty do not automatically devise intelligent ways for the students to use laptops in class. After all, this technology did not arise to solve any curricular or teaching or learning problem; nor does it help meet any particular learning objective except computer literacy.

Clemson University has implemented a successful universitywide laptop mandate, which it started phasing in as of fall 2002. The favor it has gained with participating students and faculty is documented in regularly collected assessment data, which is summarized in Chapter One. The secret to the success of this mandate, we believe, is the Laptop Faculty Development Program, which ensures that faculty interested in teaching with laptops receive forty hours of training before they take on a laptop course. The focus of the training is not on the technology but on *teaching effectively* with it; in fact, most of the hours concentrate on pedagogy. Clemson is among the very few American universities with such a faculty requirement.[1] Individual consultation time and technical support are also readily available. Almost all the faculty coming out of this program change their teaching *style* as well as their technology. Specifically, their classes become more student-active, student-centered, and student-engaging than ever before. As a result, the class conduct problems associated with laptops (Web surfing, e-mailing) almost disappear.

Some of the more creative and effective laptop faculty are showcased in the chapters of this volume. They represent all faculty ranks and the full range of disciplines, from music to mathematics. They address not only the triumphs and efficiencies of teaching with laptops but also the sometimes daunting challenges of integrating laptops effectively into their classes, the technological glitches, and the additional course preparation and creative energy required. Most of the authors also share evidence of the impact of their efforts on student attitudes and learning. In the concluding chapter,

David Brown, a laptop pioneer and a leader in higher education, gives an outside expert's assessment of how varying degrees of instructional technology can expand learning opportunities, how laptops specifically can enhance learning, and how fully the pedagogical innovations presented in this volume exploit the laptop's potential.

Linda B. Nilson
Barbara E. Weaver
Editors

Note

1. Among the top twenty public universities, the University of Florida offered a faculty laptop program from fall 1999 through spring 2001. In exchange for a free laptop, faculty were required to complete sixteen hours of training, including only four hours on "using laptops effectively," which may or may not have addressed pedagogy (http://www.coe.ufl.edu/NCATE/Documents/Tech-FacDevelopment.html and http://www.coe.ufl.edu/NCATE/Standard5.htm).

LINDA B. NILSON *is founding director of the Office of Teaching Effectiveness and Innovation, which co-oversees the Laptop Faculty Development Program, at Clemson University.*

BARBARA E. WEAVER *is program manager for Clemson University's laptop faculty development and taught the first laptop sections of several English and communication studies courses at Clemson.*

1

*This chapter describes Clemson University's Laptop
Faculty Development Program and its assessment,
offering the program as one model for designing faculty
development to successfully implement laptop mandates.
The chapter also acquaints readers with the many types
of in-class, laptop-based activities that meet best-practice
criteria for effective teaching.*

Laptops in Class: What Are They Good For? What Can You Do with Them?

Barbara E. Weaver, Linda B. Nilson

A number of North American colleges and universities are launching or considering laptop mandates for their students (see http://www.wcmo.edu/wc_users/homepages/staff/brownr/NoteBookList.html for a current list of about 180 universities with laptop or notebook computer initiatives), in the expectation that faculty will devise intelligent ways for the students to use them in class as well as outside. Many faculty regard these mandates with skepticism, if not cynicism, for several good reasons. Although students no doubt learn to use laptops, the skills involved are little different from those needed on a desktop, and they may be outmoded by the time students graduate and obtain employment. Furthermore, laptop mandates have not arisen in response to any major curricular change or teaching or learning problem; nor do they help meet any particular learning objective. All they might help are information technology budgets (Olsen, 2001).

As a result, classroom use of laptops has suffered an inauspicious beginning. In universities with a laptop mandate, few faculty have integrated the machines into their classroom teaching (Olsen, 2002), and many of those who have tried became disillusioned with the amount of Web surfing, e-mailing, and cheating going on in class (Mangan, 2001; "Georgia System Ends Laptop Program . . . ," 2001). Some schools have sought to reduce these problems with restrictive software, and some, such as Duke University, have decided entirely against laptops because of not only these problems but others as well: the additional expense for students, the prospect of preparing the faculty, and the dearth of evidence that laptops enhance learning (Olsen, 2002).

This volume makes a strong case that laptop skeptics should look again, that very good things *can and do* happen with laptops in the classroom. Each chapter between the introduction and the concluding comments features a success story in a discipline, and some in multiple courses, at Clemson University. They address the costs and difficulties of integrating laptops effectively into classroom teaching, in particular the time spent in faculty training, the hours of additional course preparation, the technological glitches, and the creative effort. Interestingly, through assessment of Clemson's Laptop Faculty Development Program we have learned that such student behavior problems as Web surfing and e-mailing almost disappear when the laptop activities truly engage the class.

What Led to Clemson's ETS-OTEI Laptop Faculty Development Program?

In fall semester 1998, Clemson University's College of Engineering and Science (CoES) began a pilot laptop program that offered one to three sections of first-year courses taught by about a dozen adventurous faculty in mathematics, computer science, chemistry, physics, general engineering, history, and English. Laptop sections of Spanish and communication studies were added as the CoES pilot developed, and faculty in business management began their own pilot program. Fall 2002 marked the end of the pilots and the beginning of a universitywide laptop mandate requiring entering freshmen in two of the five colleges to buy and bring their own laptops to campus. Two more colleges took up the mandate in fall 2003, and the fifth in fall 2004.

We believed that, with appropriate training in laptop technology and pedagogy, faculty could make innovative and intelligent student-active use of laptops. We hoped that students would be more engaged and motivated to work harder, would have the chance to interact better with the instructor, and ultimately would learn more. These hopes indeed inspired the Laptop Faculty Development Program at Clemson University, a unit set up in June 2002 under two well-established departments, Educational Technology Services (ETS) and Office of Teaching Effectiveness and Innovation (OTEI). The idea of one unit answering to two departments might make a bureaucrat faint, but it works. ETS and OTEI play nonoverlapping roles, ensuring the best that is possible in both technology and pedagogy respectively. Over the years, these units have collaborated quite smoothly on many projects and have freely shared staff and other resources. OTEI also performs various assessment functions for ETS.

What Does Successful Laptop Faculty Development Include?

Each academic year, the provost has earmarked a modest amount of funding to award laptops to faculty who want to teach a new or existing laptop course and agree to fully participate in the program. A committee makes the awards on the basis of the overall quality, practicality, and immediacy of the faculty member's laptop-teaching plan. The requirements are not superficial. Faculty commit to forty hours of training, and they are required to give back to the program by participating in the laptop faculty and student assessment surveys, leading workshops, giving presentations, writing articles, and participating in other forms of disseminating needed knowledge in this new field.

The pedagogy workshops are interdisciplinary communities of faculty (four to six) who explore laptop pedagogy together. Following the required six weeks, many of these communities elect to continue meeting weekly because they find the support beneficial in many ways. They continue to explore pedagogically sound use of laptops in conjunction with other technology and begin shifting their teaching styles from traditional lecture to more student-centered approaches relying on interaction, participation, collaboration, and hands-on experience.

The laptop pedagogy communities initiated and facilitated by the Laptop Faculty Development Program provide a collaborative climate through which participating faculty coauthor papers, develop presentations they give together at conferences, and create cross-discipline laptop assignments. Faculty also attend other workshops during the academic year that they deem of greatest use to them. They have dozens to choose from, including ETS technology workshops, OTEI teaching workshops, and laptop pedagogy symposia with demonstrations by experienced laptop faculty. They also visit at least a few classes conducted by experienced laptop faculty and discuss their observations in the laptop pedagogy communities to help shape their use of laptops in class.

Graduate students employed in the Laptop Faculty Development Program offer technical expertise to help faculty realize their vision for laptop use with students. The work of these employees has ranged from simply helping faculty get familiar with their laptops to Web site development, from teaching faculty how to use new software or hardware to developing complex interactive online class materials. Additionally, these graduate students and the program manager make hundreds of office "house calls" each year to give laptop faculty technical support and pedagogical advice at an individual level of need.

How Can We Assess Laptop Faculty Development? What Are the Results?

From its inception, the Laptop Faculty Development Program assumed a crucial assessment function. Performance measures include tracking attendance and meeting dates of laptop pedagogy communities, attendance at additional ETS and OTEI technology and pedagogy workshops, and participant evaluations of those events, as well as the number and quality of collaborative projects, major innovations, publications, presentations, and program responses to faculty and student needs.

Near the end of each semester, a laptop faculty and student survey targets laptop courses taught by faculty who participated in the program. The student items reflect our hopes for the program: Did students feel more engaged in this laptop class than they did in their other traditionally taught classes? Did they think the laptop helped them learn more? Did they sense they interacted better with the instructor? Did they believe they worked harder? Did they feel inadequately prepared to do the laptop assignments? Most of the faculty items roughly paralleled those for the students: Did they think their students were more engaged? learning more with the laptops? interacting better? Did they believe they taught differently (presumably more student-actively) with laptops than in traditional courses? Did they feel prepared by virtue of their training to teach with laptops? The results of these surveys continue to inform the program's next steps, notably what more it can do for faculty and students to enhance the teaching and learning value of laptops in the classroom.

We conducted the survey of faculty and students in nineteen laptop courses taught in fall 2002, spring 2003, and spring 2004. Some of those courses had multiple sections, and some were taught for more than one semester. Seventeen faculty members participated in the survey; several of them covered more than one course or section. The number of students who participated was 616. All the responses were confidential and anonymous.

We learned from the survey results that most students and faculty agree that students are more engaged and learn more in their laptop classes than in their traditionally taught classes. Sixty-one percent of students reported that they were more engaged, while 86 percent of faculty reported students were more engaged. Forty-eight percent of students reported they learned more in the laptop course than in traditional courses, with only 13 percent saying they learned less in their laptop course. Seventy-five percent of faculty reported that their laptop students learned more.

Faculty and students also agreed that faculty-student interaction was not hampered by using laptops in class (58 percent of students reported no difference, and 48 percent of faculty reported their interaction actually improved with laptop students). We also learned that students do not think they work harder in laptop classes (59 percent reported no difference). They reported that the convenience of a laptop—for example, always knowing where to find the online class materials and being able to upload assignments—made class work easier, and hands-on activities in class with the instructor there to help made complex course content easier to learn. Other students, who reported increased difficulty with a laptop course, made clear their problems stemmed from lack of computer skills or technical problems with their laptops. Most faculty members (91 percent) reported they did change their teaching style, and they largely felt prepared to teach their laptop course (77 percent).

The survey made clear that some students (14 percent) are not as proficient with computer technology as might be expected. In response to this finding, ETS established a student technology training task force to solve the problem. The task force developed a CD-ROM of technical tutorials that was distributed to freshmen and transfer students during the summer orientation and a checklist of technical tasks and references available through a freshman portal on Clemson's homepage. Throughout the two days before classes begin, ETS staff members meet with freshmen and transfer students one-on-one to ensure that each student's laptop is set up and working properly and that each student has the working knowledge of basic computing needed to be successful as of the first day of class. Once a student successfully completes the ETS session, an "ETS Approved" sticker is put on the student's laptop to alert faculty that the student and the laptop are ready for laptop assignments in class.

What Can We Do with Laptops in Class?

The *real* question requires more elaboration: What can we do with laptops in class that (1) has genuine learning value for students (is interactive, participatory, experiential, or hands-on) and (2) cannot be done as well or at all without a laptop, at least not in class? In fact, many of the laptop activities suggested here could be done as homework on any kind of Internet-linked computer. So why not just assign computer activities to be done out of class and forget about laptops?

According to Walvoord and Anderson (1998), one guaranteed way to enhance students' understanding is to use homework as their first exposure to new material, typically in a reading assignment, and then focus class time on the interactive-processing part of the learning, during which students apply, analyze, synthesize, and evaluate the material. Laptops lend themselves well to such activities. In-class computing activities bring other learning opportunities as well: students working under the instructor's guidance; small groups working under controlled conditions; synchronous, whole-class activities (for example, a simulation); active-learning experiences that would be impossible in reality (dangerous or costly labs); and immediate exchange of and feedback on answers, solutions, and information.

Eight categories of in-class laptop activities meet both the conditions we have set. Where appropriate, we mention which chapter(s) in this volume illustrate the application. Many of the proposed activities are just obvious possibilities that reflect general best practices in teaching.

Student-Data Collection. Laptops make it easy to collect information and responses from students in a variety of ways, and to display them to the class if desired. The survey tool on any of the leading course management systems (CMS) allows anonymous collection. If student identity is useful or relevant, an instructor can choose from e-mail; a CMS testing or assignment collecting tool; or, to make student postings public, a CMS discussion board.

What data might be worth gathering?

- Virtual first-day index cards with personal information, major, career aspiration, reason for taking the course, expectations of the course, and so on
- Class survey of opinions, attitudes, beliefs, experiences, reactions to the readings, and so forth
- Classroom assessment data, such as ungraded quizzes, the Muddiest Point, the One-Minute Paper, and the like
- Reactions or questions *as they arise* during a video, demonstration, lecture, guest speaker, or class activity
- Student feedback on peer presentations
- Midsemester feedback on the course or teaching methods

The many institutions that have placed forms for student assessment of instructor online (Sorenson and Johnson, 2003) also stand to benefit. Laptops in the classroom promise to restore the high student response rate found with paper forms.

Student Assessment. Objective in-class tests given on laptops encourage electronic cheating unless we can monitor students judiciously. This means having plenty of proctors or a network computer environment with sophisticated security software. However, it is safe and convenient to administer some online forms of student assessment in class (practice test, low-stakes quiz, open-book or open-note test, collaborative group quiz, nonformulaic essay test). Low-stakes quizzes, especially if given daily, help ensure that students do the assigned reading for the day. For such accountability purposes, an "essay test" can mean just a short paragraph summarizing, reacting to, or answering a question on the readings. Group quizzes not only assess but also make students think and talk about the material. These forms of assessment render cheating unnecessary, too difficult, or not worth the effort.

Student *Self*-Assessment. The Web offers a variety of instruments measuring personal characteristics, abilities, and preferences, not all of which are fanciful time-wasters. Some may actually increase student self-understanding and complement the subject matter of the course. Here are just a few respectable instruments that are free (unless otherwise indicated):

- Learning styles and preferences (go to http://www.clemson.edu/OTEI/links/styles.htm for links to a variety of such instruments)
- Personality and temperament, using the Keirsey Temperament Sorter (http://www.advisorteam.com/user/ktsintro1.asp)
- Career-relevant aptitudes (http://www.careerkey.org/english)
- IQ (http://web.tickle.com/tests/uiq)
- Political ideology (http://www.digitalronin.f2s.com/politicalcompass/index.html)
- Leadership (http://connect.tickle.com/search/websearch.html?query=leadership has links to several such instruments, most of which involve an expense)

Student Research. With the resources of the Internet at their fingertips, students can conduct documentary, experimental, and survey analysis and even do field research using laptops in class; a number of Clemson University faculty have used laptops this way. History professor James Burns breaks his Western Civilization classes into small groups that research topics on the Web and report their major findings to the rest of the class. He defines the topics and, for the sake of efficiency, suggests high-quality scholarly Web sites for the students to explore. In their General Engineering courses (see Chapter Eight in this volume), Matthew W. Ohland and Elizabeth A. Stephan send their students to the Web to research physical parameters and the effect of problem constraints. Their students also use motion sensors to collect data on vibration, pH response, force versus displacement, and other phenomena in real time; they then use Microsoft Excel to analyze the data.

In his Advanced Experimental Psychology course (see Chapter Two), Benjamin R. Stephens has his students use customized online systems to design and execute their own experimental research projects, using themselves as subjects. They then write up their results and electronically exchange papers, serving as reviewers for one another. In Ellen Granberg's Introductory Sociology (see Chapter Six), students access and analyze General Social Survey data, made available on the Web by the National Opinion Research Corporation (NORC) at www.icpsr.umich.edu/gss. The site even offers statistical applets for easy analysis. Finally, biology professor William M. Surver and his colleagues are redesigning several courses so that students will research solutions to complex real-world problems on their laptops, as well as collect and analyze data from laboratories broadcast live from remote locations.

Faculty in any discipline will find scholarly research resources in the collections at these sites: http://www.merlot.org/Home.po, http://www.uwm.edu/Dept/CIE/AOP/LO_collections.html, and http://www.clemson.edu/OTEI/links/subject.htm.

Before seeking their *own* Web resources for in-class or out-of-class research, students may do well to learn first how to evaluate them. A site that links to ways to assess Web sites for scientific value and validity is http://www.clemson.edu/OTEI/links/evaluating.htm.

Field research is yet another activity that laptops make easier, more efficient, and more immediate. This volume has chapters on two such examples. Glenn Birrenkott, Jean A. Bertrand, and Brian Bolt pride themselves in giving their Animal and Veterinary Sciences students a hands-on education, so they conduct many of their classes at various university farms. It has been a challenge to figure out how to carry and use laptops in such dusty, wet, and remote locations, but they have succeeded, allowing their students to measure and evaluate the growth, milk production, economic value, and income-production points of various animals, all on location (see Chapter Seven). Although normally in the classroom, Barbara E. Weaver has taken her English classes to the South Carolina Botanical Garden; students identify and chronicle locations where nature and technology collide (see Chapter Nine). Finally, in Applied Economics and Statistics Rose Martinez-Dawson has sent her students into local supermarkets to conduct price-comparison research.

Simulated Experiences. Laptops make it easy to give students a virtual learning experience under the instructor's guidance. An example featured in this volume is Paul Hyden's application of Excel simulations and demonstrations to illustrate abstract concepts in his business statistics class (see Chapter Four).

Instructors can find elaborate computer simulations on CD-ROM or the Web in many disciplines: the Business Strategy Game, Decide, Marketplace, the Global Supply Chain Management Simulation, and the Manufacturing Management Lab (developed by Clemson University professor Larry LaForge; http://people.clemson.edu/~rllafg/mmlhome.htm), all for business; SimCity for urban planning; Whose Mummy Is It? for ancient history; Unnatural Selection for biology and environmental studies; and SimIlse and SimWorld for political science and environmental studies, to name just a few.

Virtual science laboratories are also available on CD-ROM and the Web (for example, http://www.abdn.ac.uk/diss/ltu/pmarston/v-lab/ for biology and geography; and http://dsd.lbl.gov/~deba/ALS.DCEE/TALKS/CHEP-meeting9–18–95/CHEP.pres.fm.html for physics, with advice on developing labs for one's own courses).

Analysis of Digitized Performances. Although other technologies can be used to play music and to view dance, dramatic, acrobatic, and athletic performances, digital technologies offer a definite advantage for the instructor—most prominently, precise control over exactly what is played or shown when—and for the students, especially regarding the quality of the recording. In his music appreciation course, Andrew Levin adds some distinct learning advantages to going digital with laptops (see his coauthored Chapter Three). Small student groups listen to selected compositions played on laptops with an ear toward answering several interpretive and analytical questions. The students discuss the music, replaying it as needed, and discover its distinctive qualities on their own. Using customized software, they upload their responses to the Web; then Levine projects all their answers to the entire class. During the discussion that follows, he can correct any faulty responses before storing them for students' future reference.

Student Collaboration. Laptops allow students to collaborate in class on assignments and problems that require them to use the Web or special software, such as an HTML/Web editor, Microsoft Word, Publisher, PowerPoint, Excel, Access, SAS, AutoCAD, Matlab, and Maple. We have already seen examples under "student research": Burns's Western Civ students conducting Web research in small groups; Stephens's Advanced Experimental Psychology students reviewing and improving each other's research papers; and Ohland and Stephan's General Engineering students working in pairs to collect and analyze data. One more Clemson example is William Moss's Advanced Calculus and Differential Equations course. He runs it as a "studio" course in which student groups spend all but the first fifteen minutes of class time solving problems in Maple. Moreover, laptops allow students to exchange and collaborate on all manner of multimedia presentations, portfolios, and other projects.

Learning Exercises. When students have laptops, the instructor is free to design or find online exercises (individual or small-group) that reinforce and apply the material. Perhaps the previous seven categories of activities qualify as valuable online exercises as well, but we have something more specific in mind here: a form of interactive practice by which students can learn on their own both during and outside of class. The clearest example in this volume comes from Roy P. Pargas's course in computer data structures. Laptops have allowed him and colleague Kenneth A. Weaver to redesign it to approximate the master-apprentice model (see Chapter Five). Pargas has his students download and manipulate applets of various data structures so they can observe and test each structure's dynamic behavior—a far better way to learn than watching the professor sketch static segments of the process on the board. Being a computer scientist, Pargas can program whatever applets he deems helpful to his students' learning. What about the rest of us?

In fact, hundreds and perhaps thousands of these learning exercises are available free on the Web. They are usually called *learning objects* (LO), a relatively new term for a variety of online learning tools and aids. They are formally defined as digital instructional resources that are reusable in a number of learning contexts. Most definitions also include the criteria that a learning object present a discrete, self-contained lesson that requires three to fifteen minutes to complete and that it contain its own learning objectives, directions, author, and date of creation (Ip, Morrison, and Currie, 2001; Beck, 2002). The most discriminating standards also require that the object be interactive (Wisconsin Online Resource Center, n.d.), a criterion that Pargas's applets meet. Within these parameters, a learning object may be quantitative or qualitative; text-based, auditory, or graphic (static or animated); or any combination thereof.

Learning objects for just about every discipline can be found in designated LO repositories. Perhaps the most famous ones are MERLOT (Multimedia Educational Resource for Learning and Online Teaching) at http://www.merlot.org and the Wisconsin Online Resource Center at http://www.wisc-online.com/index.htm. Project Interactivate offers a rich variety of learning objects for the sciences and mathematics; it is at http://www.shodor.org/interactivate. Information Technology Services at Brock University in Ontario, Canada, displays its in-house-created learning objects at http://www.brocku.ca/learningobjects/flash_content/index.html. There are repositories of repositories, hosted by the University of Texas at San Antonio at http://elearning.utsa.edu/guides/LO-repositories.htm and the University of Wisconsin at Milwaukee at http://www.uwm.edu/Dept/CIE/OP/LO_collections.html.

Learning objects are also scattered around the Web for specialized top-ics, such as biology, nursing, and bioengineering, at http://www.cellsalive.com and optics at http://micro.magnet.fsu.edu/primer/java/scienceopticsu/powersof10/index.html.

Conclusions

Our survey findings and the teaching innovations of the Clemson University laptop faculty clearly show that laptops can provide the impetus for instruc-tors to make their classes more student-active, thereby increasing student engagement and learning. These benefits can accrue without sacrificing the quality of student-instructor interaction or adding to the student workload. But they do not automatically accompany laptop use; nor can laptops trans-form a poor instructor into a good one. Rather the benefits flow from *fac-ulty* involvement, commitment, and effort, specifically:

Active participation in both technology and pedagogical training
Willingness to change aspects of their teaching style and formats—in par-ticular, to move toward a studio, master-apprentice, interactive, hands-on, discovery-based, experiential, or collaborative model of teaching and learning (obviously more challenging in a large class)
Willingness and ability to invest considerable time in developing pedagog-ically sound and student-engaging laptop assignments, exercises, and projects

The faculty who developed the innovative, pedagogically valuable uses of laptops featured in this volume displayed all these essential qualities from the start.

We emphasize these demanding requirements imposed on faculty to caution laptop advocates who may look to technology for easy, time-saving solutions. But we also advise the naysayers that they'd better look again. Laptops are not just another glitzy technological toy. They can make good things happen in the classroom and enhance learning in ways that no other current technology can.

References

Beck, R. J. "Object-Oriented Content: Importance, Benefits, and Costs." *EDUCAUSE 2002 Proceedings,* 2002. Retrieved May 11, 2004, from http://www.educause.edu/asp/doclib/abstract.asp?ID=EDU0297.

"Georgia System Ends Laptop Program with Debt and Claims of Success." *Chronicle of Higher Education,* June 1, 2001, p. A27.

Ip, A., Morrison, I., and Currie, M. "What Is a Learning Object, Technically?" *WebNet2001 Conference Proceedings,* 2001. Retrieved May 12, 2004, from http://users.tpg.com.au/adslfrcf/lo/learningObject(WebNet2001).pdf.

Mangan, K. S. "Business Schools, Fed up with Internet Use During Classes, Force Students to Log off." *Chronicle of Higher Education,* Sept. 7, 2001, p. A43.

Olsen, F. "Chapel Hill Seeks Best Role for Students' Laptops." *Chronicle of Higher Education,* Sept. 21, 2001, p. A31.

Olsen, F. "Duke U. Decides Against Requiring Freshmen to Own Laptops." *Chronicle of Higher Education,* Jan. 11, 2002, p. A44.

Sorenson, D. L., and Johnson, T. D. (eds.). *Online Student Ratings of Instruction.* New Directions in Teaching and Learning, no. 96. San Francisco: Jossey-Bass, 2003.

Walvoord, B. E., and Anderson, V. J. *Effective Grading: A Tool for Learning and Assessment.* San Francisco: Jossey-Bass, 1998.

Wisconsin Online Resource Center. "Learning Objects." n.d. Retrieved May 11, 2004, from http://www.wisc-online.com/about/Learning%20Objects%20Def%20Q%20 Stand%20Uses.htm.

BARBARA E. WEAVER *manages Clemson University's Laptop Faculty Development Program.*

LINDA B. NILSON *is founding director of Clemson University's Office of Teaching Effectiveness and Innovation.*

2

This chapter describes an undergraduate psychology research methods course in which laptops facilitated online organization, electronic portfolios, and flexible laboratories to improve student engagement, capability, and understanding.

Laptops in Psychology: Conducting Flexible In-Class Research and Writing Laboratories

Benjamin R. Stephens

This chapter details how laptops were used to enhance a required Research Methods course in psychology. One set of enhancements was organizational. Students actively organized information, materials, and assignments on the course Web site during class. They also used laptops to facilitate organizing and constructing digital portfolios during brief class sessions for updating and revision. Laptops also allowed integration and flexible scheduling of in-class research and report-writing laboratories during class and lab meetings. Student understanding and engagement seemed enhanced by these laptop activities, and instructor-student interaction markedly increased throughout all phases of the experience. With modification, these laptop-based methods transferred well into a pilot module for an Introductory Psychology laboratory course. No doubt they can be applied more broadly to enrich courses with flexible research and communication activities.

Here, I first describe the Research Methods course that I taught without laptops for nearly twenty years, with all its shortcomings. Next I share my observations on how introducing laptops enhanced the course organization, research activities, and writing activities. Finally, I explain how these techniques will be extended to new required freshman and senior courses in the coming year.

NEW DIRECTIONS FOR TEACHING AND LEARNING, no. 101, Spring 2005 © Wiley Periodicals, Inc.

The Research Methods Class

The Research Methods course I targeted in my Laptop Faculty Development Program proposal is a basic requirement in psychology curricula. The four-credit class is a small section (twenty students) with traditional lecture-and-discussion meetings and one weekly lab meeting (ten students in each lab section). Designed for sophomores and juniors, it requires both Introductory Psychology and Experimental Psychology (a statistical methods course) as prerequisites. It aims to furnish a broad working knowledge of psychological science, methods, experimental design, and professional communication skills. The capstone assignment is an independent, original, empirical research project developed and conducted by each student.

As with most laboratory courses in the sciences, this course typically segregates teaching methods: the lecture covers conceptual topics, and the lab demonstrates methodology with hands-on activities. This segregation stems from the fact that the hands-on activities require equipment, computing resources, and dedicated space for data collection and statistical analysis; so those activities are consigned to the laboratory meetings. Scientific report writing is typically introduced in either lecture or lab, and the student then completes the report independently, often as homework.

The equipment and space requirements of a typical laboratory in the sciences create an artificial and often counterproductive separation of discussion, exploratory activities, and writing. A more natural, constructivist learning process suggests mentored, student-centered sequencing of learning experiences in which discussion, exploration, and communication tasks are selected according to the needs and timing of the learning goals (Kardash and Wallace, 2001; Gardner, 1992). I proposed using the laptops to erase the artificial lecture-lab division and let each learning experience occur as the students' needs indicated.

As I soon found out, this integration of discussion, research, and communication across lecture and laboratory time periods permitted easier transactions among the various activities and effectively eliminated the lecture-lab dichotomy. I also found that the laptop organizational improvements associated with online course development supported this integration, since relevant materials were readily available.

Laptop Organization

In addition to technically orienting faculty to the laptop, the Laptop Faculty Development Program promoted using course Web sites to organize and communicate information, materials, and assignments. Knowing nothing about site creation, I attended an HTML workshop and easily set up crude sites for my nonlaptop and laptop course. I used a hierarchical site structure because it seemed "natural" and simple to construct. It reflects a typical structure (Lazar, 2003) and mirrored my thinking as I organized course material.

Exhibit 2.1A. Entry Web Page: Syllabus

Course Description
Course Requirements
Course Grading Weights
Course Rules and Regs
University Course Policies
Course Reading
Course Calendar → (link to interactive Course Calendar)
Office Hours and Contact

Exhibit 2.1B. Course Calendar Web Page

Date	Topic	Read	Due	Lab
1/9	Intro → (link to outline) Scientific Method	Chapter 1 Demo		Open
1/14	Basics	Chapter 6 +/−	Homework	Design Experiment 1
1/16	Control	Chapter 7	Homework	Design Experiment 1
1/21	Two groups	Chapter 8	Homework	Data Collect
1/23	Applications	Style	Topic 1	Data Collect

Exhibit 2.1, in three parts, comprises linked Web pages that together illustrate the site structure for my Research Methods course. The first page, illustrated in Exhibit 2.1A, represents the Web site entry and contains hyperlinks to the main elements of the syllabus. For example, clicking on Course Calendar takes the student to the dated listing of class events shown in Exhibit 2.1B.

The course calendar was the most extensive and effective organizational tool of the site. For each date, the calendar listed the topic for class discussion, the reading for that meeting, assignments due, and the topic for laboratory meetings. Most entries in the calendar were also linked to additional materials and sites. The Demo link under the Read column, for example, gave access to an online face discrimination experiment that students could explore before conducting it themselves. In addition, each discussion topic linked to a Web page containing a topical outline, as illustrated in Exhibit 2.1C. Even some discussion points linked to supporting or illustrative material. For example, in Exhibit 2.1C, clicking on Views of a Single Study led to an external Web site on a survey of undergraduate views of party schools.

For each class meeting, my displaying the online calendar was the opening event. The calendar served as a visual cue for where we had been and where we were going; I then used it to link to the outline or demonstration of the day. I also had the freedom to navigate to other appropriate pages according to the needs and flow of the discussion or activity.

Exhibit 2.1C. Outline "Intro" Web Page

Introduction to Elements of Research
Views Across Several Studies
Views of a Single Study → (link to external site)
Theory
Hypothesis
Variables
Operational Definitions
Method
  Design
  Controls
Results
  Description
  Inference
Interpretation

Both my in-class observations and student comments documented how the laptop enhanced the course organization and structure as well as student engagement. I observed a high percentage of students following the flow of the material on their own laptops. In addition, many of them copied Web pages to serve as an outline for entering their own notes. Students' comments during the semester indicated that they found the online organization to be useful and helpful. For example, they spontaneously and frequently described the online technique as easier to follow; having a hands-on feel; and being helpful, easy to access, and easy to modify for their notes.

Why were results so positive? I suspect that part of the reason was that the Web site housed all course material in a centralized, reliable location, facilitating information transfer. As instructor, I too found the material easy to use and update. I often linked newspaper accounts and other current event artifacts to the site moments before a class or lab meeting to connect the course material to real-world events.

More subtle reasons for the positive response to the online course information emerged as the semester progressed. First, the Web site structure was familiar. But I also began to realize that the site allowed students to actively organize the course and its materials—actively because they were *navigating* as they followed along during class and lab, and at home. I suspect that they actively reconstructed the course organization each time they went through the site. This active engagement in material is a hallmark of effective learning (Brown, Campione, Webber, and McGilley, 1992; Gardner, 1992; Vygotsky, 1978).

Digital Class Portfolios

The Laptop Faculty Development Program also fostered interest in reflective digital portfolios as learning and assessment techniques. The portfolio is a collection of a student's work, selected from a larger archive of work, on which the student has reflected. Yancey (2001) posited three processes in developing this type of portfolio: collection, selection, and reflection. She argues that reflection gives students responsibility for documenting and interpreting their own learning; the communication exercise consequently promotes constructive learning and deeper understanding (Yancey, 1998). These processes are consistent with prevailing cognitive theory and principles, such as an apprenticeship model of cognitive development and assessment (Gardner, 1992), as well as socially mediated cognition that is domain specific (Brown, Campione, Webber, and McGilley, 1992; Vygotsky, 1978). These cognitive viewpoints suggest that mentored examination of self-defined achievement, as in a reflective portfolio, is fertile ground for developing deeper critical thinking skills, which are central learning outcomes in the Research Methods course. Since the students write frequently during the course, they should benefit from a portfolio requirement.

Indeed, reflective portfolios may share pedagogical elements common to proven techniques for effective undergraduate science education. This common pedagogy may enhance the value of the portfolio for the Research Methods student. Consider the similarities between portfolios and undergraduate research experiences. Research experiences effectively promote understanding and interest in science by way of the student's active involvement in an original inquiry (Boyer Commission on Educating Undergraduates in the Research University, 1998; National Science Foundation, 1996), leading to critical thinking in a mentored context suitable for effective pedagogical strategies (Kardash, 2000). The portfolio activities are also active, authentic, and goal-oriented. As in data collection for research, students collect evidence of their learning for the portfolio. As in hypothesis formation and evaluation, selection in a portfolio requires data organization as well as data assessment on conceptual and logical grounds. Finally, theoretical synthesis and evaluation resemble reflection because in both a student weighs and integrates the collected evidence to construct new understanding. Thus the reflective portfolio simply extends the learning objectives of the Research Methods course.

The laptop facilitated the construction of a digital portfolio in two ways. First, it became easier to save and organize materials, as students were required to collect their writing and related artifacts in a Web-based folder. These artifacts included all writing assignments as well as forms and materials from the independent projects. We began reviewing and organizing these collections in the middle of the semester to identify themes and prepare for reflective processing. The final portfolio required the students to integrate their reflections into themes, values acquired, and lessons learned.

Second, for the writing task laptops enabled multiple in-class sessions (ten to twenty minutes) throughout the semester to update collection of artifacts, organize and select themes, and construct the digital reflective presentation. As with the research and writing laboratories (discussed later), increased in-class interaction during these sessions seemed to

improve students' understanding of the portfolio and their sense of effi-
cacy, and it gave me the chance to show my concern for their learning.

The final portfolios demonstrated that students were able to identify
and document learning themes in their work. Many offered reflective pieces
that highlighted the improved understanding accompanying higher-quality
written reports. Most students seemed to sense the synergistic interplay
between understanding and communication. Several portfolios connected
their new understanding to external artifacts, such as advertisements in the
media or shaky claims in publicized scientific reports. The portfolios
showed evidence of their ability to think critically and conveyed a sense of
the students' excitement and competence.

Research and Writing Laboratories

In the previous nonlaptop versions of the Research Methods course, we typically conducted three experiments during laboratory meetings prior to the
independent research project. The students collaborated in groups on
the first three experiments, each of which depicts a type of psychological
research. Each experiment led to a written report, in which students were
required to communicate the experimental results in a standardized scientific style. In these nonlaptop versions of the class, the laboratory meetings
were often devoted to data collection and statistical analysis, and the writing
tasks were completed mainly out of class. With the laptop, the research and
writing laboratories were flexibly scheduled and integrated across class
and laboratory meetings.

Research Laboratories. Because the laptop served as a research work-
station, our laboratory sections met in a regular classroom. Students
designed, collected data for, and analyzed the results of the experimental
research projects using laptops during class and laboratory meeting times.
They collated and summarized the observations using Excel and word-
processed a written report of each experiment. Thus we were free to conduct discussions and these activities across class and lab times.

One of our research laboratories examined visual discrimination of
schematic faces. After reviewing the background research for the experiment in class, we conducted a preliminary experiment, illustrated in the
composite Figure 2.1. The first panel, Figure 2.1A, shows the four pairs of
schematic face stimuli. In each pair, one version of the face is configured
correctly, and the other version incorrectly. Two of the pairs are complex
faces, and the other two pairs are simple faces shaped like a Ping-Pong pad-
dle. Two sets are in normal contrast, and two sets are in reversed contrast.
Each student selected one pair for the preliminary test. During the test, students used their laptops to present the selected pair, as depicted in Figure
2.1B. While maintaining fixation on the "X," each student indicated which
face was correct. The location of the "X" was also a variable, ranging from
very near the faces (0.0 degrees of eccentricity) to very far from the faces
(40 degrees of eccentricity).

Figure 2.1. Stimuli, Display, and Data for Face Discrimination Experiment

2.1A. Stimulus Pairs

2.1B. Display

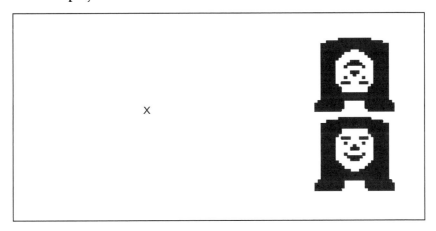

After discussing methodological concepts as they applied to the experimental protocol, we reviewed results from the literature, as depicted in Figure 2.1C (Ward, Stephens, and Dannemiller, 2003). Students compared their preliminary results to the literature, identified several potential hypotheses for the class experiment, and then developed and refined a complete experimental protocol. Next, students collected extensive data, compiling them into a single file by e-mailing copies of their data sets. They then used their laptops to calculate relevant statistics and prepared the data for presentation. After reviewing the results in class, students began to draft reports of the experiment in a series of brief writing laboratories.

Figure 2.1. (Continued) Stimuli, Display, and Data for Face Discrimination Experiment

2.1C. Typical Results

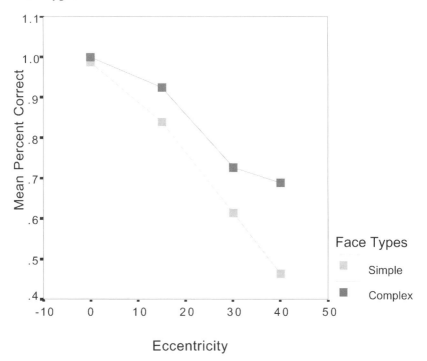

Writing Laboratories. In nonlaptop versions of the Research Methods course, I explained the report requirements in class, and the students wrote their reports as homework. Few scheduled one-on-one sessions for assistance. This minimal level of instructor-student interaction hindered students' ability to meet the communication learning objectives of the course. With laptops, however, students were able to write during class and lab meeting times, while I moved around the room to answer questions and review drafts.

For the face discrimination laboratory report, for example, we conducted two writing laboratories: a draft preparation session and a draft revision session. For the draft preparation session, I first described in class the general guidelines for a report; then each student began a fifteen-minute laptop session to outline the report, translating the general guidelines into all or some of the report subsections. As the students worked, I roamed the room. Laptops allowed them to replay the experiment and retrieve their notes.

Students completed a draft of the report out of class, but they edited it during a thirty-minute revision session. Again, I roamed the room, peering over shoulders, reading sections, and helping with additional questions running the gamut of content and style issues in scientific reporting.

Similarly, laptops made writing the capstone independent project easier, with an outline writing session and a revision session. Laptops also facilitated a peer review exercise (Libarkin and Menke, 2001). After I described the goals and requirements of peer review, each student e-mailed the penultimate draft of his or her project report to a randomly selected classmate. To start, students used the laptops to "skim and react," generating questions and concerns. In the next two sessions, they outlined and revised their reviews, which they then e-mailed to the authors.

Views on Laptop Laboratories. The entire process for the face discrimination experiment consumed roughly three weeks, with no artificial segregation of the content into class versus lab meetings. At times, the class moved back and forth through the elements of the research and writing process, revisiting our discussions of methods, goals, and other key topics. I observed students in the writing process behaving like professionals in one-on-one office conferences, resolving questions of clarification, content, and style and producing better scientific reports as a result. Student comments and ratings supported these observations. Compared to other psychology classes (including my previous nonlaptop sections), students rated this laptop course more favorably on interaction, feedback, and teaching in general. These ratings were bolstered by written comments about the instructor. Students saw me as willing to help, concerned about their learning, clear in communicating both content and my expectations, and even energetic, fun, and exciting. I believe that the enhanced instructor-student interaction that research and writing laboratories allowed largely explained the students' positive assessments of the course.

Future Laptop Courses: Introductory and Senior Psychology Laboratories

These laptop experiences in Research Methods have supported our department's decision to institute two new one-credit-hour laptop laboratory courses, each required of all majors. These courses would not be possible without the practical and pedagogical benefits associated with laptop classes. For freshmen, we have created the Introductory Psychology Laboratory. Here, students will conduct several demonstration experiments and communicate these experiences in brief written reports and a laboratory portfolio. In the Senior Laboratory, students will construct a reflective program portfolio.

Before developing the first course, we wanted to determine if the laptop pedagogy used so successfully in Research Methods would work with introductory-level students, so we conducted a pilot lab module with a nonlaptop honors section of Introductory Psychology. The class (twenty-three students) met in a desktop computer lab to simulate a laptop class. The

Exhibit 2.2. Scoring Outline for Pilot Introductory Lab Reports

Compared to the understanding and knowledge of a typical "B-average" Introductory Psychology (Research Methods) student, the report shows that the student author understands much less (less, etc.) than the typical target student about the following elements of psychological science:

1 Much less	*2 Less*	*3 Slightly less*
4 Slightly more	*5 More*	*6 Much more*

1. Theory
2. Hypothesis
3. Rationale
4. Variable and operational definition
5. Methodology
6. Data analysis
7. Interpretation and critical thinking
8. External validity
9. Internal validity
10. Scientific writing

module was similar to the face discrimination experiment described earlier. After a brief presentation of background material, students constructed their own hypothesis, collected data online, analyzed the results descriptively using Excel, and completed a written report of the experiment. The class was engaged in this task for three consecutive seventy-five-minute meetings. Attendance was nearly 100 percent despite the fact that the experience was extra-credit only and the reports would not be graded. Nonetheless, gauged against the skills and knowledge of the typical introductory-level student, the reports were impressive. I even verified my impressions by having a senior who'd taken Research Methods rate the reports. Specifically, he was asked to rate the author's apparent understanding of ten main elements of research methodology, using the rubric in Exhibit 2.2. He rated each report twice on each element: first, the author's understanding compared to a "B-average" Introductory Psychology student; and second, the author's understanding compared to a B-average Research Methods student. The senior's ratings varied between "slightly more" and "more" knowledge than the typical B-average introductory student for eight elements. The other two elements ranged from "slightly more" to "slightly less." The ratings were between "somewhat less" and "less" knowledge than the typical B-average Research Methods student for six elements, but the other four elements ranged between "slightly more" and "slightly less."

To summarize these results, the introductory-level authors scored as well as the Research Methods students on four elements and better than typical Introductory Psychology students on eight elements. These evaluations suggest that the module was an effective technique for enhancing scientific understanding at the introductory level. However, since the class was an honors section of introductory psychology, the effectiveness may be limited to more talented students.

We have not conducted a pilot study to determine the potential effectiveness of the Senior Laboratory, in which students will construct a program digital portfolio. However, if portfolios worked so effectively in Research Methods, they should work just as well in the Senior Laboratory program. We suspect that improved instructor-student interaction, which laptops promote, is integral to an effective capstone experience such as the Senior Laboratory. Since the topic of the portfolio is student-centered (focused on the individual student's understandings, experiences, and values), we expect it will accomplish its learning goal of improving the students' sense of breadth and connectedness across the curriculum.

Final Views

For me, the appeal of laptops goes beyond undergraduate coursework. Laptops enabled me to better implement the constructivist approach, which is believed to be most promising in promoting understanding, interest, and commitment to science and scientific careers (Boyer Commission on Educating Undergraduates in the Research University, 1998; National Science Foundation, 1996). In this approach, students learn research in authentic hands-on activities (data collection, hypothesis formation) designed to develop "situated cognition," which is the ability to represent and reason about specific phenomena and processes (National Research Council, 1999). These learning experiences improve students' understanding, which in turn promotes a sense of competence and, in the research context, generates a sense of discovery and excitement (Kardash, 2000).

In my class, laptops enhanced the fundamental context for constructivist learning: faculty-student interaction. They also enabled flexible scheduling of a variety of class activities, allowing the learning process to be student-centered rather than driven by logistical boundaries between lecture and lab time. Finally, they helped to set the tone by providing a more transparent course structure as well as better tools for the students to organize and transmit course materials and the artifacts of their learning. As a result, students seemed to acquire deeper understanding, a stronger sense of self-efficacy, and feelings of engagement and satisfaction in their work, empowering them with the confidence they need to enjoy science and perhaps pursue scientific careers.

References

Boyer Commission on Educating Undergraduates in the Research University. "Reinventing Undergraduate Education: A Blueprint for America's Research Universities, 1998." Retrieved June 6, 2004, from http://naples.cc.sunysb.edu/Pres/boyer.nsf.

Brown, A., Campione, J., Webber, L., and McGilley, K. "Interactive Learning Environments: A New Look at Assessment and Instruction." In B. Gifford and M. O'Conner (eds.), *Changing Assessments: Alternative Views of Aptitude, Achievement, and Instruction.* Boston: Kluwer, 1992.

Gardner, H. "Assessment in Context: The Alternative to Standardized Testing." In B. Gifford and M. O'Conner (eds.), *Changing Assessments: Alternative Views of Aptitude, Achievement, and Instruction.* Boston: Kluwer, 1992.

Kardash, C. M. "Evaluations of an Undergraduate Research Experience: Perceptions of Undergraduate Interns and Their Faculty Mentors." *Journal of Educational Psychology,* 2000, *92*(1), 191–201.

Kardash, C. M., and Wallace, M. L. "The Perceptions of Science Classes Survey: What Undergraduate Science Reform Efforts Really Need to Address." *Journal of Educational Psychology,* 2001, *93*(1), 199–210.

Lazar, J. "The World Wide Web." In J. A. Jacko and A. Sears (eds.), *The Human-Computer Interaction Handbook: Fundamentals, Evolving Technologies and Emerging Applications.* Hillsdale, N.J.: Erlbaum, 2003.

Libarkin, J. C., and Menke, R. "Students Teaching Students: Peer Training in Undergraduate Education." *Journal of College Science Teaching,* 2001, *31*(4), 235–239.

National Research Council. *How People Learn: Brain, Mind, Experience, and School.* Washington, D.C.: National Academy Press, 1999.

National Science Foundation. *Shaping the Future: New Expectations for Undergraduate Education in Science, Mathematics, Engineering, and Technology.* Arlington, Va.: National Science Foundation, 1996.

Ward, A. W., Stephens, B. R., and Dannemiller, J. L. "Adult Perception of Schematic Faces That Infants Prefer." (Abstract.) *Journal of Vision,* 2003, *3*(9), 833a. Retrieved June 6, 2004, from http://journalofvision.org/3/9/833.

Vygotsky, L. *Mind in Society.* Cambridge, Mass.: Harvard University Press, 1978.

Yancey, K. *Reflection in the Writing Classroom.* Logan: Utah State University Press, 1998.

Yancey, K. "Student Digital Portfolios." In B. Cambridge (ed.), *Electronic Portfolios: Emerging Practices in Student, Faculty and Institutional Learning.* Washington, D.C.: American Association of Higher Education, 2001.

BENJAMIN R. STEPHENS is associate professor of psychology and his department's undergraduate coordinator at Clemson University.

3

A particularly innovative use of laptops is to enhance the music appreciation experience. Group listening and discussion, in combination with a new Web-based application, lead to deeper understanding of classical music.

Appreciating Music: An Active Approach

Andrew R. Levin, Roy P. Pargas, with Joshua Austin

Music appreciation is traditionally taught as a lecture or lecture-and-demonstration course. The students first learn the building blocks, the so-called elements of music (melody, harmony, and so on). After establishing a common language and set of concepts, the professor then progresses chronologically from earliest times to the present, presenting the works of acknowledged masters. The music is presented in the context of music history, art history, political and social history, biography, and geography.

Students also study the music itself, listening for the elements of music. Before playing a piece of music, the instructor prepares the students for what they are about to hear. They then listen to the piece over a class stereo component system, with the instructor occasionally describing the music while it is playing. Finally, the instructor reviews the music and asks for student reactions. (All current music appreciation textbooks are supplemented by CD recordings of the works discussed in the text.)

Music appreciation has been presented in this manner for generations; it can be quite successful, especially given a good textbook, good musical selections, and a charismatic instructor. The successful instructor engages the students, helping them "participate" in the listening of music and not simply hear the music passively.

Note: Because this chapter focuses on application of a new technology to a pedagogical problem, the instructor of the course, Andrew R. Levin, is the primary author. The Appendix, written by the software manager, Roy P. Pargas, describes the technology developed.

NEW DIRECTIONS FOR TEACHING AND LEARNING, no. 101, Spring 2005 © Wiley Periodicals, Inc.

Disadvantages of the Traditional Model

Instructors do not always succeed in making the music come alive for the students. Since it is difficult to evaluate the students' understanding of the music itself, lecture content and exams often focus on the academics of music—history, biography, and politics—rather than on the music itself. One common method to test students' understanding of musical content is to require them to identify music selections. Another is to have them evaluate a passage vis-à-vis the elements of music. However, this technique is generally used at the start of the semester while studying the elements; it might not be continued in later exams. As a result of these simple tasks, students often develop only superficial listening skills and become passive learners and listeners. In a music class, one would hope it is the music itself that receives primary attention.

It should be noted that students who generally perform well academically also succeed with the more objective content of this course, even if they have little or no musical background. Again, though, this type of achievement does not address a student's understanding of the music itself. For that, she must be taught *how* to listen and be given guided opportunities to develop the skill. Whereas many professors are successful in teaching good listening skills, I have developed a system that emphasizes development of these skills with the result that students truly gain understanding of the music itself, not just of the (admittedly important) academic matter of history and biography. In addition, this system uses laptop computers in a classroom setting.

What Is Needed

Music appreciation can become a more successful course if certain activities are added.

Repeated Listening in Class. Most teachers of music appreciation agree that repeated listening is essential to greater understanding of music. However, this is not often done in class; it is usually relegated to out-of-class study time. Professors usually play works just once (if that often), and they do not always instruct the student on *how* to listen.

Continued Dialogue with Major Concepts. Students require regular and guided practice with terminology and concepts as they relate to the music itself. Whereas professors focus on these concepts early in the semester, they turn their focus to more academic topics as the semester progresses.

Group Activity. Students often strengthen their understanding of concepts by practicing them, by actively discussing and defending their understanding of music. Such discussion, in small groups and with guidance from the professor, helps students develop these concepts. To ensure proper understanding of the concepts, the teacher then reviews and expounds on the students' conclusions.

Modeling. It is necessary for the instructor to model good listening skills, showing students how to listen to and evaluate the music (as opposed to simply *telling* the students what to listen for).

The New Ideal: A New Way to Teach Appreciation

A new ideal, then, for teachers to shoot for poses three goals: (1) the students learn how to listen, (2) they gain deeper understanding of the music itself, and (3) they also learn the objective content associated with the music (composer biographies, the history and politics of the times).

How are these goals accomplished in an actual music appreciation course? I have developed a process that I find to be successful. In it, the teacher and students progress through seven steps, described next.

Brief Introduction. The professor gives a short introduction to the day's musical selection. Rather than rehashing material from the book, the teacher presents just enough content to pique the students' interest and direct their listening.

Specific Listening Assignments. Students are assembled into small groups (usually set for the entire semester or unit of study), assigned music to listen to, and shown how to focus their listening. For example, one group might listen to tracks 1 and 2 and then discuss harmony and rhythm, while another group listens to tracks 3 and 4, focusing on melody and form. Alternatively, all groups might listen to the same excerpt, though they may focus on different concepts. The possibilities are endless, with the actual musical content dictating possible approaches.

Listening. Students then listen to their assigned excerpts, using their laptops as media players, taking notes as they see fit.

Discussion. After listening to their short excerpts, group members discuss what they heard, focusing on the elements they were assigned. They can also listen again to a section in the music to refresh their auditory memory.

Sharing. One person in each group then posts the group's comments to a common access point. This could be a discussion board of a given course management system, or a specially developed Web-based application, as is the case with MusicGrid, new software developed at Clemson University.

Review. The instructor then reviews each posting, commenting on the students' insights. The review process is also an opportunity for repeated listening, to clarify further any issue at hand.

A Final Hearing. After hearing the work in small pieces, the students finally listen to it in its entirety, enabling them to grasp the whole of the work.

Hesitations About Using This Method

As reasonable as this method sounds, there are many who would object to it. The primary concern is the length of time given to listening and group discussion at the expense of traditional lecture—the dissemination of content. Some instructors also argue against their loss of control over the content and method of the class.

It is quite true that the professor spends less time presenting content. Is this necessarily bad? Is it only through lecture that students learn material? My students are still responsible for material in the text, and I assist them by providing study guides, lists of questions about material I consider important. Contrary to my initial expectations, on exams students performed just as well on the objective content as they ever had, even though I spent less class time on this material. I now take it as a given that students are perfectly capable of learning objective content and displaying their understanding on exams. What they are *less* capable of is understanding the music itself; it is for this reason that I have changed the focus of my course from objective content to musical understanding.

I might also suggest that this method puts an instructor's ego to the test. Many instructors enjoy the role of professor as Font of Knowledge, whereas they are less comfortable in the role of professor as Facilitator, although the latter can afford greater learning opportunities and foster independence of thought.

Then there is the (usual) trouble with laptops. Even given the lofty goals presented here, students are still creatures of today's society and are easily seduced by high technology, in this case laptop computers. These expensive toys create problems regarding inappropriate use—an issue familiar to laptop teachers. For the most part, though, I find my students are engaged in their activities, and to whatever degree they are distracted I have not found it detrimental to the class as a whole.

But no matter how responsibly my students act, one area requires their attention: the necessity for them to attend class fully prepared. With reference to technology, this means bringing a fully functioning laptop to class along with headphones and audio CDs. If a student forgets his materials, he does not participate in the discussion while he catches up, listening to music the others have already listened to. I recommend penalizing students who do not bring their materials to class, with clear guidelines and consequences noted in the syllabus.

The Benefits

Teaching music appreciation in this manner brings a number of benefits. Some of them are identified here.

Understanding of Concepts. Students are compelled to apply the concepts and terminology they learned at the start of the course to each new piece they encounter. As they continue to use these concepts, their understanding of them deepens.

Solving Puzzles. These group discussions appeal to students who enjoy solving puzzles. Rather than being told (by an "expert") what the music means, students are asked to come to their own conclusions regarding specific portions of music and in a limited, though reasonable, time frame. It is an attainable goal, one that gives students a feeling of accomplishment when achieved.

Depth Versus Breadth. In a traditional music appreciation course, students often gain a broad understanding of music, yet they delve deeply into a work only if they feel a particular connection with it. It is not common to listen repeatedly and deeply in such a class. By contrast, this laptop method amounts to a regular opportunity for deep listening, albeit for just a short section of the music. Students have the chance to examine every piece they study at a deep level.

Exams. It is a pleasure to observe students discovering new pieces of music. It is even more rewarding when they successfully demonstrate their increased understanding on an exam. Compared to my students in previous nonlaptop classes, those in my laptop class clearly show greater understanding of music on their exams, though it is difficult to determine the exact cause of the difference.

One way to test musical understanding and awareness is for students to identify not only the musical selection they are listening to but also which *section* of that piece is being played. The sections of a work can be quite distinct from one another, or quite similar. Part of appreciating music is understanding the function of the various sections of the music and how they relate to the whole; it is thus important for students to identify particular sections of a work. The students in the laptop class demonstrated greater ability to identify sections of a piece than have students in previous semesters. I attribute this to their better listening skills and their ability to make memorable distinctions between the sections. Whereas in previous semesters I asked students to identify entire works, or perhaps one of two or three larger sections of a work, in the laptop class I asked students to identify up to eight sections of a piece. Their degree of accuracy in answering these questions was astounding. Of course, I worked to develop this skill in them by first having them identify just a few sections earlier in the semester and then building up the challenge to more complex pieces as the semester progressed.

One of my concerns was whether students would perform well on the objective questions on these exams, given the reduction in class time on these subjects. I need not have been concerned. Laptop students answered these questions just as well as had students in previous nonlaptop classes.

Scheduling Laptop Usage

I have taught the laptop version of the Music Appreciation course on Tuesdays and Thursdays for seventy-five minutes each. Teaching it in any less time would be unreasonable, given the time it takes to go through the seven steps listed here.

I required students to bring their laptops only on Thursdays. On Tuesdays I taught in a traditional lecture-and-demonstration mode, and on

Thursdays we used the laptops. I did this for a few reasons. First, two learning modes afforded variety for the students, keeping the class experiences fresh. (It also saved them the effort of toting around their laptops for every class session.) Second, the lecture day gave me the opportunity to model good listening habits. Third, it allowed me to choose which mode best suited the individual pieces of music. Finally, regardless of the day, I could administer tests on paper, *not* on the laptops. Until secure testing environments exist online, I will rely on the time-honored paper test.

Two Methods of Teaching with a Laptop

Central to this method of teaching music appreciation is the ability to post the results of group discussion to an accessible location. One is the discussion board feature found in course management systems such as BlackBoard and WebCT (I used MyCLE in my course, a course management system developed at Clemson University, though BlackBoard is now replacing it.) The second is a newly developed Web-based application called MusicGrid, which allows all postings to appear on screen on a single grid or table. The first system is available at schools that license a course management system; the second is still in development but will be available for general use soon. (See Appendix for more information.)

Discussion Boards. To make best use of the discussion board, the instructor creates new discussion topics before each day's class. Typically, each section of music gets its own topic. Students are then assigned topics and told where to place their comments. After all students have posted, the professor reads each entry, perhaps plays the music again, and comments on the responses. The student posts are then available for the rest of the semester as a resource.

One important disadvantage to this technology is that entries once posted cannot be altered (at least not in MyCLE). This limitation reduces their integrity and value for later study and reference. BlackBoard allows entries to be edited, but only by the original author. If using this course management system, an instructor who recommends students alter their posts has no guarantee they will do it, or do it accurately.

Another disadvantage of discussion boards is the inability to view more than one entry at a time. This makes it difficult to compare the entries of a group. Moreover, it is impossible to view how a single element might change across the sections of the music.

MusicGrid. It was with these difficulties in mind that I pursued a new solution. I collaborated with Clemson computer science professor Roy P. Pargas in developing a Web-based application that built on the strengths of the discussion board but allowed online editing and simultaneous display of many groups' responses. With assistance from Clemson computer science undergraduate Josh Austin, MusicGrid was created, creating an ideal laptop environment for a music appreciation class.

MusicGrid is built on a database (see details in Appendix). As students post to it, their comments are added to the database. These entries are then displayed in a single grid or table that students can view on their own laptop. The professor can also view the grid and even project it to a screen at the front of class. In this way, she can review the student comments while also making necessary edits.

For my needs, I listed the elements of music across the top row and the various sections of the piece down the first column. This basic grid allowed a variety of learning activities. For instance, during one class period the students determined how harmony was developed throughout a piece, and their responses were displayed in a single column underneath the header "Harmony." During other class periods, the students focused on a single section of music, but with each group commenting on different elements. This arrangement resulted in a series of table cells filled out horizontally. The possibilities are, of course, endless.

Another advantage of MusicGrid over discussion boards is the instructor's ability to edit content after it has been posted. This way he can note and correct inaccuracies in the students' observations, making the posted content suitable for students to study later.

A final feature of MusicGrid is the option for the instructor to "freeze" the contents of a given grid, eliminating the possibility of students' tampering with a corrected grid.

Evaluation of the Laptop Method

Is the laptop method of teaching music appreciation more effective than the traditional method? Certain survey results and my own observations, which I have already shared, suggest it is. The survey collected both closed-ended responses and open-ended comments from my Music Appreciation students at the end of the spring 2004 semester. The closed-ended items offered a five-point scale: strongly agree, agree, no difference, disagree, and strongly disagree. Variations from this scale are noted.

Some of the results were quite predictable, though others were surprising in how they supported or seemed not to support the effectiveness of this method. Many instructors believe the best approach to teaching music appreciation is having a supposed expert (the instructor) telling students just what the music contains. They would be surprised by the degree to which the students felt they developed their listening skills while working with less-expert peers. To the statement "Working in groups helped me refine my listening skills," 21.4 percent strongly agreed, 75.0 percent agreed, and the remaining 3.6 percent claimed no difference. No students disagreed.

It is also widely assumed that most students do not like group activities, but I did not find this to be the case. In response to the statement "I enjoy working in small groups," 35.7 percent strongly agreed, 53.6 percent agreed, 10.7 percent had no opinion, and again none disagreed.

I was concerned that sacrificing lecture time to listening and group time would negatively affect the students' music appreciation experience. In response to whether students thought it a good trade-off, especially considering that much of the exam would be based on objective material, their response to the statement "By necessity, spending more time in group and laptop activities means spending less time covering content from the textbook; I found this to be a good trade-off" was surprising. There was strong agreement from 21.4 percent, 60.7 percent agreed, 14.3 percent had no opinion, and only 3.6 percent disagreed, none strongly.

My teaching strategy was an equal mix of laptop activities and lecture with demonstration. Given the interest in technology among today's youth, it may not be surprising that, in response to the statement "The mode that I enjoyed the most was . . . ," 64.3 percent responded "with the laptop," 21.4 percent "in lecture/demonstration," and 28.5 percent no preference.

Given the students' preference for technology, I was surprised by the responses to the next two statements. Students didn't seem to think that the method made much difference in how well they came to understand the music. To "Overall, I feel that traditional lecture/demonstrations are effective in increasing my understanding of the music," 14.3 percent strongly agreed, 67.8 percent agreed, 10.7 percent had no opinion, and 7.2 percent disagreed. To "Overall, I found using laptops increased my understanding of the music," the results were almost identical: 17.9 percent strongly agreed, 67.8 percent agreed, 10.7 percent had no opinion, and 3.6 percent disagreed.

My department chair and I both felt the laptop course was successful enough to warrant offering it again. Meanwhile, MusicGrid continues in development, with its second version, suitable for all disciplines, coming out by mid-2005 under the name MessageGrid.

Final Thoughts

To be quite honest, when I first considered laptop teaching I had difficulty finding a way to incorporate it into courses that I taught. Laptops seemed like a solution in search of a problem. However, after attending many workshops and symposia, speaking with other laptop faculty, and observing their classes, I found this new method forming in my mind. Although the particulars are still in development, I think the overall concept is effective in teaching music appreciation and in holding student interest. It cannot stand as the Only Way to teach the subject, but I offer it as a highly useful alternative. It is my hope that this method will not only benefit my students but also inspire my colleagues in music to develop similarly effective laptop pedagogies.

Appendix: The Technology of MusicGrid

A course called Online Systems was developed and has been taught at Clemson University's Department of Computer Science over the past three years. The course is taught at the senior undergraduate and first-year-graduate level. In a semester-long assignment, students design and implement a major project. Some of the projects undertaken have led to conference publication or pending submission to conferences. Among them are projects that developed a laptop-based computer science course, a Web-based authoring tool for online questionnaires and surveys, a server-based algorithm for fluorescent diffusion tomography, online review sessions for a laptop-based computer science course, and a Web-based attendance checker using card swipes. This course is fertile ground for innovative applications, and students aggressively work toward conducting publishable research.

In the spring 2004 semester, I redesigned the course to use four technologies:

1. Web server: Microsoft IIS
2. Database: Microsoft SQL Server
3. Programming environment/language: Microsoft VisualStudio.NET, C#
4. Operating system: Windows XP Professional

These applications are deployed on Clemson University's Department of Computer Science Microsoft IIS Web server accessing the department's MS SQL Server. All of this software is already available to the department because of its continuing membership in the MS Developer's Network Academic Alliance (MSDN AA).

In MusicGrid, the instructor collects student responses to questions through an ASP.Net Web-based application running on a Microsoft IIS Web server. The responses are saved into an SQL Server database and can be viewed by the students through their browser during class. The instructor can display the table containing all student responses on a projection screen in order to stimulate discussion. She can also critique, annotate, and correct student responses. At the end of the period, students download the table for future review.

MusicGrid is currently in development. Now in its second major version under the name MessageGrid, it can be adapted to a variety of disciplines. This work has been supported by a grant from the 2003 Microsoft Curriculum and Content Program and a faculty fellowship from the ETS-OTEI Laptop Faculty Development Program of Clemson University. For more information, contact Roy P. Pargas at teech@clemson.edu.

ANDREW R. LEVIN is associate professor of music and the orchestra conductor at Clemson University.

ROY P. PARGAS is associate professor of computer science at Clemson University.

JOSHUA AUSTIN graduated from Clemson University in June 2004 with a major in computer science.

4

This chapter reports on a mathematics professor's experience leveraging laptops in a required intermediate statistics course with a challenging student population. Use of laptops streamlined course delivery, enhanced classroom interaction, and improved both his students' and his own overall course experience.

Teaching Statistics by Taking Advantage of the Laptop's Ubiquity

Paul Hyden

Laptops have come to play a vital supporting role in managing and delivering my undergraduate courses since I saw them improve my course delivery, my rapport with the class, and the student learning experience. I experimented with laptops and observed the effect of their usage in a required intermediate course in business statistics and probability. The course serves all levels of undergraduates in the College of Business and Behavioral Science at Clemson University. The student population is challenging, with many students openly admitting their predisposed anxiety and hostility toward the subject.

The unique opportunities that laptops afford made it easier for me to reach them. Student access to computers simplified my teaching life, freeing me to focus on and improve my relationship with the class. Laptops also helped me express the best in my own teaching personality. Around-the-clock availability, portability, and personal accessibility make student laptops a unique enabler of powerful instructional techniques.

This chapter describes how I managed my students' use of laptops in class and how the technology advanced my educational goals. It closes with my assessment of the limitations of the technology and the course changes I'm making to take fuller advantage of the laptop's potential to enhance teaching and learning.

My Goals for Technology

Three major goals guide how I implement technology in my classes. First, I strive to create a community of learning among the students and myself. Indeed, students respond positively when they can establish relationships with peers as well as the instructor, and I have found that laptops can enhance those interactions. Second, I want student input to drive the daily direction of the course, within the confines of my syllabus. Matching what is addressed in class to student needs makes class time productive and relevant to students, and both synchronous and asynchronous online communication enable me to tailor my course content daily. Finally, I want any technology I might use to reinforce and support learning rather than define and control it; I quickly discovered that laptops do this seamlessly, just like textbooks and chalkboards. My hope is that, once the novelty of the laptop wears off, labeling my course a "laptop course" will sound as ridiculous as calling a course with a textbook a "book course."

A course driven by student input and a firm sense of community frees me from the typical patterns of delivering information to students. I can foster two-way communication in the classroom—not just from instructor to student but from student to instructor and from student to student in a fluid and dynamic network, one that mimics how information flows within the Internet. As the instructor, I act simply as a centralized node directing this network of learning, rather than its sole source of knowledge. In this environment, I find that students are less likely to target their frustration at me and more likely to seek out solutions on their own than they are in the traditional classroom hierarchy.

In my mind, a course structured around a learning community and student needs requires high attendance at class, no matter what kind of technology is used. Therefore I keep attendance and enforce a strict attendance policy with serious penalties after a reasonable number of absences.

Discussion Board Postings

Discussion boards, which are now a common virtual environment in course management systems, allow students to submit their own questions and answer the questions of other students. Unlike chat and e-mail, a discussion board makes all postings visible to both the instructor and the entire class. This tool proved useful in inducing my students to do the textbook readings that I assigned for almost every class. With each reading, students were to post either a novel question or an answer to another student's question on the assigned material before the next class.

Before using laptops, I had students turn in a handwritten question that was based on their reading assignment. This served several purposes. First, it motivated students to do the readings when due. Second, it helped them transform their frustration with the material into specific queries and confusions that I could help them address. Finally, it saved class time in taking attendance. But this approach had some negative effects as well. For one, these daily question submissions led students to expect me to compose a specific, individual response for every question, which was not feasible. So when the inevitable frustration with the material surfaced, I was an easy target.

Further, the daily questions generated a stack of papers that absorbed significant time and attention in every class. In addition, the stronger students in the class complained because they didn't always have an honest question to ask about the readings. So even though the initial low-tech approach served its purposes well enough, the class and I both paid a price.

The laptops improved the daily question assignment and added several benefits the paper version couldn't match. First of all, since I could read the student questions before class, I was able to tailor the class time to clear up confusion raised on the discussion board. If students posted their question soon enough, I answered it before class, enabling them to make a higher-quality contribution in class. Second, with all the questions and responses visible to the entire class, struggling students benefited from seeing the answers to more than just their own question. They realized that other students faced the same struggles they did and felt more comfortable with their own difficulty. No doubt, too, students wrote higher-quality postings because they were subject to public scrutiny, and better postings were more likely to get an answer. Third, the stronger students, freed from having to make up a question just to satisfy the assignment, seemed to enjoy the chance to help their peers and apply the material they mastered. In addition, their answers left me with fewer questions to address myself. Fourth, the questions I did answer were rarely unique, and I could broadcast a uniform response to several related questions that students could read at their convenience. As a by-product of all these practical benefits, the traditional hierarchical classroom structure was replaced by a network community of learners.

Daily Online Quizzes

In addition to posting on the discussion board, students were required to complete a daily online quiz based on their reading assignment prior to the next class. Before I began using a course management system that made this online tool available, I conducted daily paper-and-pencil quizzes in class. They induced most students to do the assignment readings, but they took away precious classroom time. They also generated more papers to grade, a tense classroom environment, and a distraction from the business of learning the material.

With the new technology, students completed the online quiz at their convenience before the beginning of the next class. This meant more class time for learning. The course management software instantly graded the quizzes and entered student scores in the course gradebook. To further defuse the stress and downplay the assessment role associated with quizzes, I also allowed students to retake the quiz as many times as they wanted, with the gradebook recording only the highest score. Under these conditions, a quiz served only to motivate students to do the reading and give them feedback about their comprehension of the new material. Many students even said that they enjoyed getting the feedback and felt more comfortable about the course content as a result. Note this total reversal in student reactions from the pencil-and-paper quiz. Being completed before class, the quiz also informed me how well the students understood the reading and how to best use my precious class time with them.

Even though I didn't administer in-class exams on laptops, I did try to make them a learning experience as well by letting students bring in their own handwritten "cheat sheets." The act of constructing such a sheet generates a lot of learning and helps students focus their studying on mastering concepts and processes rather than memorizing formulas.

With all the exam and quiz results in the gradebook, students also tracked their progress throughout the semester on their own time and followed up with me when their performance fell short of their expectations.

Laptops in Class: A Computer Lab on Demand

Demonstrating mathematical phenomena and problem solutions in class is a basic teaching method in mathematics, and I usually conducted such demonstrations projecting the images from the instructor's classroom computer to the class. Three principles guided my computer demonstrations. First, I wanted to display concepts that I could not simply write on the board. I didn't view the computer just as an electronic archive for a static set of notes. Second, I wanted to concentrate on a few key ideas and not squeeze in too many, or distract students with flashy but shallow content. Third, I wanted to keep the tools of my presentation simple and conceptually focused. So I confined most of my demonstrations to Excel, which was widely available and already familiar to some of my students. The other students at least gained exposure to the spreadsheet program, which they would be learning in their business courses sooner or later.

Laptops in the classroom helped me solve a problem that I had encountered in the past when my demonstrations relied solely on projected images. Just watching the screen, my students couldn't follow what I was doing, in part because of their limited experience with the software I used. But integrating laptop activities into my demonstrations made learning easier for my students.

Making Random Variables Concrete. The challenge of teaching the concept of a random variable immediately suggested using laptops in the classroom. In nontechnical terms, a random variable is a number associated with an occurrence of a random experiment. Hence, it is both a variable in that it can take on many values, and it is random because the actual value it takes on is not known until it is observed. The common notation we use for a particular random variable is X, while the notation x is used to refer to an observation of the random variable X.

Many of my students still struggle with the concept of a variable, and the idea that an unknown value can also be random often generates a lot of confusion. Probability instructors use physical objects such as dice to describe random variables, but they are limited by the fact that every possible roll of a die has the same probability, and values cannot be customized to an arbitrary probability distribution. Students instinctively pick up on these points where an example is lacking, and they can misapply the concept because of it.

To make this theoretical notion of random variables concrete, I showed the class how to build a simple random variable using functions in Excel. (In an earlier class, I introduced the students to Excel by leading them through some simple exercises.) Specifically, students constructed an arbitrary discrete random variable. They then observed the random variable with each press of a button, getting a feel for what it means for a variable to be random. They continued to play with the variable to see how closely their observations matched the distribution of the random variable.

Laptops helped me make a related key concept concrete as well: the mean of a random variable. If we take a sample of observations of a random variable and compute the average, the resulting value will converge to the mean of the random variable as the sample size increases. The laptops, doing what computers do best, generated samples of thousands of observations of the random variable, allowing the students to observe convergence to the mean in real terms for actual observations of the random variable.

Computing Expected Value and Variance. Students don't appreciate how useful a formula is unless you can show them how much time they can save by using it. However, demonstrating this convincingly at the chalkboard is extremely time-consuming and still fails to show the full power of the result. After I had slowly modeled the computation at the chalkboard, the class and I used Excel to compute the expected value and variance of a random variable. Then we created a new random variable that was a linear transformation of the previous random variable. Again, we went through the steps for computing the expectation and variance of the new random variable. At that point, I demonstrated that the simple laws of expected value and variance produced the same values as the much more taxing work of computing the expected value and variance directly from the random variable. To drive the point home, I changed the values used in constructing the new random variable, demonstrating that the laws of expectation and variance really did work as advertised for arbitrary coefficients on the new random variable. Even though I still used the chalkboard to show the conceptual steps in applying the result, Excel actually demonstrated the powerful applicability of the laws.

Limitations and Improvements Needed

Laptop technology and the human memory being what they are, not all the students had a functioning laptop with them when it was needed. Fortunately, I designed all my in-class laptop activities for small groups, and each group was in charge of ensuring that one member brought a working laptop to class each day it was needed. But strictly individual in-class exercises would be hampered by reliance on laptops.

Before the laptop class, it didn't occur to me to build graded assessment into the in-class demonstration exercises, but the students questioned their relevance given that they were neither graded nor tested directly on exams. My future course offerings will include a graded element in these exercises.

Some improvements I would like to see are out of my hands. The discussion board in course management software would benefit from a new feature allowing both the instructor and the students to evaluate postings with a numerical score. These ratings would furnish feedback to students and allow the instructor to mark which responses students should note the most. In addition, the tool archiving the postings actually stores responses only in one place, as they first appear, even if they relate directly to later iterations of the topic.

In any case, technology is not a cure-all. I am excited about leveraging it creatively to deliver dynamic, relevant course content, but I do not always use it. Concepts must drive the choice of technology, not the other way around, and some concepts can actually be obscured by computers. During the unit on hypothesis testing, for example, we spend a lot of time working through examples at the board. In fact, whenever I want the students to focus on a thought process and not a computation, I have them put away their laptops. I too still spend plenty of time at the board with chalk in hand, talking with students. However, technology ensures that the time I do spend at the board is more focused and dynamically adjusted to the needs of the students.

PAUL HYDEN *is assistant professor of mathematical sciences at Clemson University.*

5

Laptops helped two faculty members adapt a highly challenging, critical computer science course to increasing enrollment. Among the course enhancements the technology made possible were daily quizzes, animation-based demonstrations and exercises, and more authentic assessment.

Laptops in Computer Science: Creating the "Learning Studio"

Roy P. Pargas, Kenneth A. Weaver

Programming is a skill, and as with all skills it is best learned through practice and exercise. Traditionally programming has been taught through lecture—that is, with the instructor up front writing segments of sample code on a blackboard and students copying down the code. Today, the availability of a laptop computer on every student's desk allows other, more effective, ways of teaching and learning in a computer science class. This chapter describes some of the possibilities, using a specific computer science class, Data Structures and Algorithms, as an example.

About the Course

Data Structures and Algorithms (CS4) is usually the third computer science course taken by majors. It is also required in many physical science and engineering programs. Normally taken in the sophomore year, it is a foundational course and a prerequisite for all junior- and senior-level computer science courses. Students study a variety of data structures, which are software components used in computer programs. They become familiar with the behavior of each structure, analyze its complexity, develop code implementing it, use the code in small applications, and learn how to combine structures into larger applications. These structures are dynamic, starting out empty and growing and shrinking as the application executes. In short, a data structure is a dynamic building block used by software developers in large projects.

Most students consider CS4 to be a difficult course. Several reasons are likely. First, the course forces students to think critically. Software development often presents two or more ways to organize a solution, usually involving competing data structures. Students must carefully analyze the various situations and contexts in which the program is to be used and decide among the approaches according to issues of space and time efficiency. The choices are rarely cut and dried.

Second, some tools that facilitate analysis are mathematical. Proof by induction and solutions of recurrence equations are two examples of powerful mathematical tools that can facilitate analysis of various software solutions to a problem. Many students have a phobia for mathematics and avoid straightforward mathematical approaches to analysis; as a result, they make choices without analysis at all.

Third, the data structures themselves are complex. Data structures are rarely simple or easy to understand. Rather, they are highly efficient software tools that have evolved over several decades, the distilled product of the minds of mathematicians and computer scientists. It takes time and patience to walk through the code that describes a structure's behavior. Some students skim impatiently through the code and mistakenly think that tracing a few values through the structure is enough to give them a thorough understanding of how a structure behaves in every situation. Only during tests or algorithm development do the impatient students realize that they missed subtle, but critical, points in the structure's behavior.

Fourth, in a large application selecting the right mix of structures and getting them to work harmoniously is difficult. Even after a student understands how each data structure behaves, selecting the right set of structures for a large application requires even more analysis and thought.

Fifth, the availability of student-teacher one-on-one time is decreasing. Over the past fifteen years, economic pressure on educational institutions has pushed the student-teacher ratio ever higher, and computer science has not been spared. In programming courses, a class size of twenty-five or fewer has been considered ideal, and thirty-five the absolute maximum. But now thirty-five to fifty students are commonly squeezed into one class, drastically reducing the amount of one-on-one time, attention, and guidance that an instructor or teaching assistant (TA) can give to any one student. At best, the student-teacher ratio will level off, but the trend will probably never reverse itself.

Therefore, how we teach problem solving and computer programming has to change. It has always been true that the best way for a student to learn and understand data structures is to work with them actively, and not just passively listen to the instructor lecture about them. But given today's realities, how can we provide this quality of instruction and guidance to students? The traditional lecture gives them no opportunity for active engagement with data structures; all they can do is listen and take notes, possibly asking a question or two. Worse yet, as class size grows, one-on-one guidance is becoming scarce. Ideally, students should apprentice in a master-apprentice setting or studio environment. Here, small groups of students actively hone their craft by performing exercises designed to teach the nuances of data structures and receive immediate feedback from the instructor or TA overseeing their work. With a laptop for every student, this master-apprentice model becomes possible (Moss, 2003).

The Way It Used to Be

For the past twenty years, CS4 has been taught in the standard, traditional format: three hours per week of lecture, conducted by an instructor (professor, lecturer, or experienced graduate student), and two hours per week of lab, led in twenty-student sections by a graduate student. The lecture is supposed to impart the theory, and the lab the practice through small and focused programming exercises. The students' theoretical knowledge is assessed through short quizzes, full-period tests, and a final examination. The instructor furnishes additional programming experience in four to six larger and more difficult programming assignments due in two to three weeks. When student enrollments were low, two lecture sections of twenty to twenty-five students, both taught by one instructor, and two or three lab sections, led by one or two graduate students, were sufficient.

Only when enrollment started to increase did problems arise. First, the lectures were not always in sync. Lecture sessions were taught by instructors with varying levels of experience. Although the teaching team (lecture and lab instructors) met once a week and had a common syllabus, instructors could not deliver the lecture content at the same rate. As a result of this uneven content delivery, students from one lecture section were less prepared for the lab exercises than students from another.

Second, the lecture sessions were of uneven quality. The department tried its best to staff CS4 lecture sections with seasoned professors, but it did not have enough experienced faculty to cover the increasing enrollment. So it filled in the blanks with adjuncts, lecturers, and graduate students, even the best of whom had to familiarize themselves with the textbook and course material.

Third, the lab sessions were also of uneven quality. They were led by TAs, mostly master's degree students in computer science who served for an average of one year. By and large, the TAs had at most one semester of experience teaching this course; then they graduated. Some new TAs were less adept in a given programming language than the students were. In addition, the TAs ran the labs without supervision. Not surprisingly, then, the quality of lab instruction was uneven and occasionally poor.

Fourth, students did not realize that they did not understand the material until it was too late. As enrollment increased, many more students who needed extra help failed to take advantage of the abundant office hours available. Since new CS4 concepts build on earlier ones, a student's problem not detected early snowballed quickly and often left her hopelessly behind. In earlier years, when enrollment was low, the instructor spotted weaker students immediately and called them in for special review sessions.

Redesigning CS4

CS4's radical redesigning started in fall 2002 with a pilot program involving one of three lecture sections and two of five lab sections, all designated "laptop sections," in which students had to bring their laptops to every class meeting. Table 5.1 shows the staffing changes through spring 2004, including introduction of undergraduates. (See Campbell and Pargas, 2003; and Herron and Pargas, 2004, for details of the redesign.) Students attend one lecture section and one lab section, and one professor is responsible for both lecture and lab.

Given the large enrollment, both lecture and lab are held in an auditorium that seats more than one hundred. Six students sit at each rectangular table. The room slopes slightly upward toward the back, so that the instructor can see students' faces over the screens of their open laptops. The instructor's desktop computer projects onto a large screen at the front of the room, and student laptops can be connected to the projector. The room has four wireless access points (two were insufficient for all the students, as we found out in fall 2004.) The problem is the lack of room between rows for an instructor or TA to squeeze through to approach a student near a wall, making responding to some questions difficult.

Student laptops allow tremendous flexibility in organizing content delivery and practice opportunities. The activities during lecture and lab, summarized in Table 5.2, permit several major pedagogical changes.

First, we can now assess student progress frequently, even daily. Students take a low-stakes, online self-assessment quiz set up on the course management system just before lecture. The quiz, covering topics from the last lecture, is available to students one hour before lecture. It is open-book and open-Web, and students may consult one another. Because the quiz is graded automatically and instantly, the instructor receives immediate feedback on how well the class understands recent class material and can adjust the day's lecture accordingly, and the students receive early feedback on how well they understand the material. Most important, a weak student can no longer hide from getting the individualized help the instructor wants to give.

Occasionally, we use this assessment tool for other purposes, too, at the end of a period to gauge how well students understood the current day's material and on new material not yet covered to gauge how much of it students already know. (See WebCT, 2003; and Blackboard, 1997–2004, for more information on using course management systems creatively.)

The second change is that we spend the first twenty to fifty minutes of class teaching new material in new ways. What is different in this laptop class, however, is that lecture is always accompanied by some form of animation (applet) demonstrating the dynamic characteristics of the data structure of the day. Students download and work with the animation and any other supporting material as the instructor lectures. Therefore students can learn the behavior of a data structure by manipulating it independently on their laptops, not just listening to or mimicking the instructor.

Table 5.1. CS4 Staffing Changes, Fall 2002 Through Spring 2004

	Fall '02	Spring '02	Fall '03	Spring '04
Instructors	3	2	1	1
Lecture sections	3	2	1	1
Lab sections	5	5	1	1
Teaching assistants	2 grad	2 grad	2 grad	2 grad, 3 undergrad
Students	98	90	65	75

Table 5.2. Distribution of Activities in CS4

	Fall 2003	Spring 2004
Self-assessment quiz	10 minutes	Just before class
Lecture	30–40 minutes	20–50 minutes
Lecture exercise (lex)	35–45 minutes	25–55 minutes
Lab session	120 minutes	120 minutes
Tests	Online, 75 minutes	Online, 120 minutes

Animations are available on the Web, and new ones are being developed every day. For an excellent example, see Gogeshvili's applet (2003) that illustrates the behavior of several tree-based data structures.

Third, to guarantee that students learn each nuance of a data structure, a carefully designed lecture exercise (called a *lex;* see Table 5.2) leads them through a variety of situations to help them uncover subtle but important behaviors. During the lex, students are encouraged to discuss and collaborate with one another; many form groups of three or four. Chances are that a confused student can learn from a neighbor. If not, the instructor and TA are available to help. Students also submit online answers to questions designed to guarantee they see specific features of the structure.

Although it would be difficult to test our hypothesis, we think our students are learning better with less lecture, fewer self-assessment quizzes, more directed activity (animations and lexes), and more peer collaboration and immediate feedback.

Fourth, we design weekly lab exercises to strengthen students' programming skills and ability to analyze algorithms. The two-hour lab gives students the chance to work with their laptops on a lab exercise more difficult and complex than a lex. As during a lex, students consult with each other, and the instructor and TAs if necessary. To guarantee high and uniform instructional quality and labs in sync with lectures, the instructor (rather than a graduate student) assumes direct responsibility for the lab, overseeing lab development, reviewing pertinent material, clarifying any unresolved issues, and delivering any new content. The graduate and undergraduate TAs are present just to assist the students. (The undergraduates are selected from the previous semester's CS4 class on the basis of not only their performance but also their personality, gender, and ethnicity. This way, all current students have at least one TA with whom they can identify.)

A fifth major pedagogical change is that we give two or three full-period tests and a three-hour final examination—all online, automatically graded, and more authentic than before. Students receive exceptionally quick performance feedback; they can also answer a small but real program development question as part of a test. This was never before possible with paper tests because program development requires access to a computer. In the past, instructors could ask for only segments of code, which they graded manually. Now instructors can assess more authentically and spend much less time grading.

Sixth, being in charge of both lecture and lab, the instructor has more flexibility. For example, since some students perform poorly on tests when pressed for time, the instructor can design a seventy-five-minute test (the length of a lecture period) but give it during the two-hour lab period. This permits reducing the length of the lab assignment and moving it to the lecture period. Similarly, if a class does poorly on a self-assessment quiz, the instructor can decide at a moment's notice to devote part of a lecture or lab to the previous lesson.

Seventh, review sessions can be conducted electronically. Once a week, the instructor holds an optional one-hour review session outside of lecture and lab. Even if he is out that week, he can still hold it electronically at a prearranged date and time using Macromedia Breeze Live (Macromedia, 2004), a software system that allows students to access a Web site and communicate with the instructor through the Internet. During these virtual meetings, students key in questions and receive text answers from the instructor at the site. All logged-on students can view the communication. Moreover, instructors and students who have a suitable camera (Web cam) connected to the computer can also see each other and communicate orally. Students without a Web cam can see other students' headshots and hear the audio but can participate only through the keyboard.

Looking to the Future

It may be too early to delineate the role of the laptop in the classroom, but we can take stock of where we are now and decide where we want to go next. Clearly, the laptop or its successor is here to stay. It is increasingly affordable even to college students and shows great instructional potential.

In computer science as well as other fields, active engagement is the most effective way for students to learn. They learn best about data structures by manipulating them to see how they work. They learn best how to program by actually programming. This is why we spent time and effort developing focused lexes. Animations and lexes, and the rich social context in which students come to understand what they represent, create a powerful learning environment, a kind of studio in which apprentices master their analytical and programming skills.

The cost of education and economic conditions being what they are, class size is unlikely to shrink and may even continue to increase. So academic institutions should take a serious look at how to better manage their most expensive resource: the faculty. They might examine ways of reorganizing delivery of course content so that a single instructor and several TAs, for example, can engage a large class of students in effective group and individual activities. We already know that an inspired instructor and a few energetic TAs with a course management system can develop a fruitful learning experience and deliver it efficiently to a large class, so long as the students have laptops.

We will continue to improve CS4's design and course material with better animations, lexes, and lab exercises. We will experiment with the number and mix of TAs to determine the best number of graduate and undergraduate assistants for a given class size. We will try a new wireless classroom—one with round, seven-foot-diameter, banquet-hall tables seating nine students and giving the instructor and TAs greater freedom of movement. We will test recitation software that allows students to submit their work electronically for class viewing and discussion. We will continue to examine whether this master-apprentice studio model does, in fact, deliver course content more effectively than lecture. Finally, we will continue to tap into and enjoy the electricity that we instructors can feel in a room full of young people actively seeking to learn.

References

Blackboard. "Integrating with the Blackboard Learning System," 1997–2004. Retrieved June 4, 2004, from http://www.blackboard.com/dev/WhyLS.htm.

Campbell, A. B., and Pargas, R. P. "Laptops in the Classroom." In *Proceedings of the ACM 34th SIGCSE Technical Symposium on Computer Science Education,* Reno, Nev., Feb. 19–22, 2003, pp. 98–102.

Gogeshvili, A. "Binary Search Tree Applet," 2003. Retrieved June 4, 2004, from http://www.cs.clemson.edu/~pargas/BST.

Herron, J., and Pargas, R. P. "Blending Technology into Review Sessions." In *Proceedings of the 15th International Conference on College Teaching and Learning,* Jacksonville, Fla., Mar. 29-Apr. 2, 2004, pp. 47–55.

Macromedia. "Creating a Meeting Using Macromedia Breeze Live," 2004. Retrieved June 4, 2004, from http://www.macromedia.com/support/breeze/live.html.

Moss, W. F. "Laptop Pedagogy," 2003. Retrieved June 4, 2004, from http://www.math.clemson.edu/~bmoss/laptop_pedagogy.

WebCT. "Learning Without Limits: Flexible E-Learning Solutions for Institutions Across the Educational Spectrum," 2003. Retrieved June 4, 2004, from http://www.webct.com/service/ViewContent?contentID=17980017.

ROY P. PARGAS is associate professor of computer science at Clemson University.

KENNETH A. WEAVER is academic advising coordinator for the Department of Computer Science at Clemson University.

This chapter describes the experience of two faculty members who implemented laptop technology in a lower-division social science course. The authors focus on the pragmatic issues associated with incorporating this technology into the social science classroom and recommend several strategies and resources.

Teaching with Laptops for the First Time: Lessons from a Social Science Classroom

Ellen Granberg, James Witte

This chapter describes how two sociology professors initially implemented laptop technology in their classrooms. In our case, this came in the form of a laptop course in which all our students had access to the Internet during class. This situation presented enormous benefits as well as significant challenges. We explain both, along with our distinct approaches to integrating laptop technology into a course, and give our limited assessment of the impact of laptop use on our students' learning outcomes.

Laptops are the latest in a series of technologies that are revolutionizing classroom teaching (Lengel, 2004b). Much of the early work incorporating computer technology into the classroom occurred in disciplines such as engineering, computer science, and mathematics (Lengel, 2004a), while humanities and social science students primarily used computers outside the classroom. Recently, however, the development of inexpensive laptop computers along with the growing availability of wireless networking has made it much more feasible to bring this technology to the social science classroom.

There are important ways in which laptop instruction in the social sciences differs from that found in disciplines such as engineering or mathematics. First, the latter are what could be called "problem-based disciplines," where many courses involve mastery of specific problems that can be adapted for software programs such as Excel, Mathematica, or AutoCAD. A second and related benefit in these disciplines is that mastering the use of specific pieces of software can contribute directly to mastery of the intellectual material presented in these courses. For example, business statistics students who complete homework assignments in Excel learn both statistical concepts and a state-of-the-art application of those concepts; further, they finish the course with a skill they can list on a résumé.

Engineering students can design prototypes on computer-assisted design packages similar to those they will use in the workplace, mastering both theory and practice in ways that relate directly to their long-term career goals. Such benefits can be a compelling reason for both students and faculty to invest the considerable resources required to incorporate laptop technology into the classroom—for students, the $2,000 to $3,000 to purchase the computer, and for faculty the time required to integrate laptops into lesson plans, homework assignments, and assessments.

Until relatively recently, such potential did not translate cleanly to the social sciences or the humanities, and as a result the expense rarely justified the benefits. Over the past several years the Internet has exploded with resources relevant to teaching sociology as well as other social sciences. (See the Appendix for a list of some of the Web sites we use most frequently.) Many of these sites have been around for years, and we both had incorporated some of them into lectures and homework assignments. Yet our use of them was frustratingly limited. On our campus, classroom access to computers for social science instruction was restricted to a relatively small number of on-campus labs, which meant our students primarily used these Web sites outside of class (say, as part of a homework assignment). In-class use usually had them watching passively while we gave demonstrations from the lectern. In both cases, the Internet's enormous potential to enhance student engagement and learning stayed in the distance.

Several advances in laptop technology have brought us today to a place where their widespread incorporation is both practical and appealing. First, they are now powerful enough to download large files quickly, an important feature for use during valuable classroom time. Second, newer laptops are small and lightweight enough that faculty can reasonably require students to bring them to class regularly. Third, they have become relatively inexpensive, allowing universities to require that incoming students purchase one before arriving on campus. (In absolute terms, of course, the extra expense can be quite burdensome for less wealthy students.)

The relatively recent availability of laptops that are powerful, fast, lightweight, and affordable represented a critical step toward bringing laptops into the social science classroom. However, their use was still somewhat limited because it remained quite difficult to get students onto the Internet during class. Harnessing the fullest potential for laptop teaching required availability of the second technology, wireless Internet access.

This access allows computers to be connected to the Internet (or a computer network) via radio waves, eliminating the need for data ports and Ethernet cables. This makes it possible for an entire class to be connected to an Internet site without any physical connection to a network. With the purchase of a small number of wireless transponders, any ordinary classroom can become a computer laboratory.

Levine (2002) has written that the true benefit of laptop technology in the classroom comes from its ability to create "two classrooms in one." When laptop lids are closed, the environment is that of a traditional classroom. With lids up, the classroom becomes a computer lab, and Levine argues that laptops enhance learning most effectively as instruction moves seamlessly between these two environments. In our experience, the widespread availability of wireless networking was essential before both environments were possible during sociological instruction.

Of course, making laptop computers and wireless networks widely available does not necessarily improve student learning. The true advantage of these technologies is the opening they give us to teach differently (Spurlin, 2003). Using somewhat dissimilar approaches, we each set about incorporating laptops into our teaching of the introductory course in sociology. In the next section, we describe our two approaches and their respective advantages and disadvantages.

Implementing Laptop Technology for the First Time: Two Experiences

We each brought our own priorities, circumstances, and levels of technological sophistication to our respective laptop courses. One of us is an untenured assistant professor and a somewhat unsophisticated technology user. The other is an associate professor who has taught courses on the Internet in society and has a specialty in online data collection methodologies. Our differing backgrounds colored our approaches to using laptops in the classroom. The untenured assistant professor, concerned with balancing teaching and research responsibilities, sought to incur minimal disruption to her existing lesson plans, resulting in a course design that included five designated "laptop days" during which students completed a graded in-class assignment that applied recent lecture material. In contrast, the tenured associate professor chose a more integrated implementation of laptop technology in which students used their laptops daily and for a variety of classroom purposes. Students were encouraged to use them to take notes and, more important, use the wireless environment. This environment was offered to the students as a means to access outside Internet resources as a real-time supplement to classroom-based activities and communicate "silently" with their peers during class. From this faculty member's point of view, students' minds often wander in the classroom, and they regularly engage in an ongoing conversation of sidelong glances, knowing looks, and discrete whispers. The aim here was to use technology to channel these normal classroom behaviors in a way that would be more efficient and perhaps less disruptive. In addition, this faculty member used periodic, planned group laptop activities not unlike those of his colleague.

Before detailing our respective approaches, we will outline the environment in which each of us taught these laptop classes. In fall 2002, Clemson University began requiring incoming engineering and science students to purchase laptops; by fall 2004, this laptop mandate was universitywide. Since laptops first appeared on campus, faculty members had the option of creating "laptop sections" in which all enrolled students were required to own a working laptop and bring it to class. During the spring 2004 semester, we were each assigned to teach one of these sections, as well as a second nonlaptop section of the same course, Introductory Sociology, with a typical enrollment of fifty students per section. In addition, prior to teaching the laptop section we each completed a series of preparatory workshops designed to facilitate our transition to laptop-based instruction.

As mentioned earlier, we chose our own strategies for implementing laptop technology in our classrooms. Here we detail those strategies and their outcomes.

Approach One: Integrated Use of Laptops

This instructor hoped to have the students use their laptops during most lectures and discussions, and to use them to access a Blackboard virtual classroom that was always "in session." The idea was to allow students to record and exchange their questions and comments in real time. The instructor's goal was to follow the discussion in real time and try to incorporate the chatter into the class. On occasions when this proved too difficult, the archive function in Blackboard allowed the faculty member to review the discussion later and address it in the next class. This instructor also used breakout groups for class discussion. Students were expected to use their laptops to ground their discussion and prepare their class presentations. Students often had to search for relevant online resources, and in these instances their report was to include URLs and other relevant resources they had found.

This integrated approach ran into some significant technological barriers. For example, though the classroom had long tables with ample workspace for students' laptops, it had only a few power plugs, which meant that students who hadn't fully charged their batteries before class needed to shut down before the ninety-minute class ended. In addition, significant limits to bandwidth hampered in-class communication at times, particularly at the start of class when many students were trying to log onto the network at the same time. Finally, the Blackboard virtual classroom application encountered problems, especially its archiving features.

None of these technological barriers were insurmountable; indeed, all shrank significantly during the semester. Nonetheless, they presented real problems for the integrative laptop approach. In particular, student buy-in, a key predictor of success for any type of instruction, was questionable at the start of the semester. Still, about one-third of the students were regular in-class laptop users, taking notes, asking others questions, and looking for relevant (and sometimes not so relevant) online materials.

Though the integrated laptop approach was not an overwhelming success, at least not in this first attempt, this effort contributed to the success of discrete, spontaneous laptop activities that sprang up both in response to student questions and when the instructor felt the class would benefit from something different from what was planned.

The instructor regularly used semester-long breakout groups of six to eight students. These groups prepared their own study guides for exams in exchange for the instructor's and researched and reported in class on special topics (for example, everyday experience with racism and prejudice). In the laptop section, students used the Internet to inform their discussion and presentation. For example, during the discussion of education as an institution in contemporary society, each group was assigned a topic from among online education, elite higher education, home schooling, vocational and technical education, the No Child Left Behind Act, and continuing education. While researching their topics, the groups circulated URLs to Internet universities, Harvard University, a Web site for home-schooling parents, a White House information page on the No Child Left Behind Act, and a local community college.

Another successful laptop exercise followed an assigned article that proposed a typology of the various ways in which religious organizations use the Internet. (Essential to the sociological method, a typology is an analytical construct used to categorize empirical social phenomena.) The typology posited three basic ways the Internet is used for religious purposes: (1) passive presentation of church information and religious content, (2) interactive exchange of church information and religious content, and (3) online worship. The groups found online examples of each use, as well as online religious materials that did not cleanly fit into the typology.

Approach Two: Discrete Use of Laptops

This approach incorporated in-class laptop activities with minimal impact on existing lecture material and course design. The instructor made lecture notes available in both PowerPoint and Word format and encouraged students to augment these notes during class. All class handouts and study guides were also distributed by way of the course management system rather than on paper.

These efforts were intended to encourage students to make regular use of their laptops and bring them to class regularly. However, the primary pedagogical use of the laptops occurred when students completed exercises designed to reinforce concepts covered during lecture (the "laptop days"). In each case, resources available on the Internet were key elements of the exercise. For example, after hearing a lecture on evaluating sources of sociological data, students surfed the Web to find examples of both unreliable ("bad") and reliable ("good") statistics about the social world. The assignment served multiple instructional purposes. First, it reinforced lecture material by having students apply it. Second, it sparked a lively discussion of the many ways in which sociological data are used to manipulate public opinion. Third, by identifying reliable statistics students often found sources of good online data that they could use in future exercises, in other classes, or for their own information.

A second exercise followed a series of lectures on components of culture, particularly values (societal standards for judging right from wrong), beliefs (what members of a society believe to be true), and norms (rules for social behavior). In preparation for this assignment, students were taught to access a Web site containing data from the General Social Survey (http://www.icpsr. umich.edu/gss; see the Appendix for details). The survey, which has been conducted almost every year since 1972, contains the opinions of a representative sample of noninstitutionalized adult Americans on a variety of issues, including abortion, drug use, politics, work and career, and beliefs about success. It is an enormously valuable tool for illustrating social science concepts ranging from political orientation to childhood socialization.

The Web site also contains a simple analytical program from which students can quickly learn to run frequencies (that is, a table with percentages) or cross-tabulations. This assignment had three components. First, students discussed what percentage of respondents would need to "agree" with a given question before it could reasonably be considered a "widely held" aspect of the culture. Second, they explored the General Social Survey Web site, examining the percentage of respondents who, for example, supported legalization of marijuana or believed success usually came to those who worked the hardest. Third, they each identified one survey question that they felt captured a widely held element of American culture. Students shared these results in class and related their findings back to the lecture material.

Laptops and Student Learning Outcomes

We chose to provide some detail about these exercises because we believe they highlight several ways in which combining laptop technology and Internet resources can benefit social science instruction. First, the Internet is a vehicle through which social science concepts can be directly applied, giving students an opportunity to test their mastery of ideas presented in lecture and their textbooks. For example, during the exercise on culture described in the previous section, students were asked to identify which element of culture their question represented. Their responses often revealed significant gaps in their understanding of these concepts and gave the instructor the opportunity to clarify the related material.

Another benefit of exercises of this kind is that they offer enormous potential for teaching critical thinking in a setting that appeals to students more than traditional venues do. During the lesson on good and bad sources of statistical data, students received a list of characteristics of reliable data and searched the Internet for examples of both good and bad data, obtaining concrete evidence for their assessments. Many students found this exercise challenging because they were often reluctant to deem a statistic unreliable, especially if its presentation looked particularly professional or it validated a personal belief they held. This furnished a powerful opportunity to illustrate the principles of critical thinking, and to help students hone their ability in this area. Further, real-time Internet access, combined with the chance for students to debate these issues as they arose, added a sense of immediacy and energy that were lacking when the same assignment was given as homework.

Given these benefits, we think laptop technology merits continued use. However, merit considerations cannot be complete without exploring how the technology affects student outcomes. The circumstances under which we taught our first laptop classes allowed us to conduct a limited field experiment. As mentioned earlier, we were each assigned to teach one laptop and one nonlaptop section of introductory sociology during the same semester. With the exception of laptop-related activities, we used the same textbook, lectures, and course materials in both sections, so we could compare the sections and make a limited assessment of their outcomes.

The students in the laptop class using a discrete approach (assignment of specific laptop days) achieved an average final grade of 86 percent, or a B. Those in the nonlaptop class conducted by the same instructor received an average final grade of 85 percent (also a B). We compared grades on midterm exams and found no significant difference there either. Even the students in the integrated laptop class (ongoing use of laptops throughout the semester) did not perform significantly better than those in the nonlaptop class on their midterm or final grades.

One likely reason laptops did not improve our students' scores was the disconnect between our teaching and our assessment instruments. Learning with laptops is a more interactive process than is traditional classroom instruction, yet we both used assessment tools such as multiple-choice exams that test memorization of detail rather than interactive mastery of concepts.

We explored the possibility that our assessments masked some of the benefits of laptop learning by comparing class performance on another kind of class assignment, one that required higher-order thinking. Students in the class using the discrete laptop approach were assigned a small project in which they identified a research question, collected and analyzed a small amount of data, and presented their results. These students had many more opportunities to analyze and discuss social research than their counterparts in the same instructor's nonlaptop section. So we might expect them to perform better on this assignment than the nonlaptop students. Indeed, the laptop-section students scored six points higher (half a letter grade) on average on this assignment than did the nonlaptop students, a statistically significant difference ($t = 3.6$, $df = 60$, $p < .001$).

Clearly this small field experiment does not definitively show that laptop technology generates better learning outcomes. If anything, it suggests how complex it can be to make such an assessment in a social science or humanities course. Further, it confirms that laptops are no different from any other technology in that it is the teaching they allow rather than their mere presence that improves student learning.

Conclusion

Our initial forays into teaching with laptops have convinced us that it has enormous potential to increase learning, particularly when combined with Internet resources. We believe that the power of the technology derives from the opportunities it creates to bring abstract, intellectual concepts to life, enliven and deepen interaction between students and instructors, and empower students to teach themselves and one another. It also contributes to one of the core goals of a social science education, creation of an educated citizenry. For these reasons and despite the sometimes significant hurdles that must be overcome, we conclude that using laptops in class can enhance both students' academic progress and their intellectual development.

Appendix: Recommended Internet Resources

The resources here may be useful for teaching sociological and other social science concepts.

http://www.icpsr.umich.edu/gss The Web site for the General Social Survey data from 1972 to 2000. It contains an application that supports analysis ranging from simple percentage tables and bar graphs to sophisticated multivariate analyses. Data downloads are available but are not necessary in using the analysis tool. The software program SDA performs the data analysis. A Web description of the software and of other data sets that use it for online analysis can be found at http://sda.berkeley.org.

http://www.fedstats.gov A portal that links users to all of the publicly available statistical data published by the federal government. Through this link students can access myriad descriptive statistics as well as raw data. The portal organizes the information in several ways, by topic, state, agency, and so on. An additional link, Data Access Tools, takes users to selected online databases maintained by federal agencies (Bureau of Justice Statistics, Bureau of Labor Statistics, U.S. Census Bureau, Bureau of Economic Analysis, and others).

http://unstats.un.org A general source of international statistics.

Useful Web sites for specific focus areas:

http://www.claritas.com A market research firm that offers, on its homepage, a link to a free Web-based program called "You Are Where You Live," a breakdown of the sociodemographic composition of every zip code in the United States; helpful for illustrating concepts such as inequality and social class.

http://www.opensecrets.org data on political funding, campaign financing, and political contributors.

http://www.prb.org Population Reference Bureau, formerly the AmeriStat Web site; sources of population data.

Web sites focused on aging and older populations:

http://www.aarpmagazine.org/ American Association of Retired Persons Magazine
http://www.aarp.org/ American Association of Retired Persons
http://www.ssa.gov/ Social Security Administration
http://www.alz.org/ Alzheimer's Association
http://www.leisureworldarizona.com/ Leisure World Community Association
http://www.nia.nih.gov/ National Institute on Aging

Web sites of formal organizations (both controversial and noncontroversial):

http://www.adl.org/adl.asp Anti-Defamation League
http://www.democrats.org U.S. Democratic Party
http://www.rnc.org U.S. Republican Party
http://www.scouting.org Boy Scouts of America
http://www.wckkkk.org White Camelia Knights of the Ku Klux Klan
http://www.sierraclub.org Sierra Club
http://www.catholic.org Catholic Online (not directly affiliated with the Vatican or the Roman Catholic Church)

References

Lengel, J. "Math Teachers," Apr. 7, 2004. Retrieved June 14, 2004a, from http://www.powertolearn.com/articles/teaching_with_technology/archive.shtml.

Lengel, J. "Wireless Networks," Jan. 16, 2004. Retrieved June 14, 2004b, from http://www.powertolearn.com/articles/teaching_with_technology/archive.shtml.

Levine, L. E. "Using Technology to Enhance the Classroom Environment." *T.H.E. Journal Online,* Jan. 2002, *26*(6). Retrieved June 8, 2004, from http://www.thejournal.com/magazine/vault/a3819.cfm.

Spurlin, J. "Evaluation of the North Carolina State University College of Engineering Mobile Computing Pilot Program." *Flashlight Case Study Series,* 2003. Retrieved June 14, 2004, from http://www.tltgroup.org/resources/F_Eval_Cases/NCSU_wireless.htm.

ELLEN GRANBERG *is assistant professor of sociology at Clemson University.*

JAMES WITTE *is associate professor of sociology at Clemson University.*

7

Teaching animal sciences, like most agricultural disciplines, requires giving students hands-on learning opportunities in remote and often computer-unfriendly sites such as animal farms. How do faculty integrate laptop use into such an environment?

Incorporating Laptop Technologies into an Animal Sciences Curriculum

Glenn Birrenkott, Jean A. Bertrand, Brian Bolt

When a land-grant university requires students to have laptops and urges faculty to teach with laptops, the traditional agriculture disciplines face challenges unlike those of other disciplines. We describe how the faculty of an animal and veterinary sciences department started incorporating wireless laptops into first-year courses and several other courses in the major, as well as how they plan to integrate the technology throughout the entire curriculum.

The First Year in First-Year Courses

The 2003–04 academic year marked the first year of participation in Clemson University's laptop program for the Department of Animal and Veterinary Sciences (AVS). As only freshmen were required to have laptops that year, only our introductory courses used the technology. One such course that introduced laptops was Orientation to Animal and Veterinary Sciences, which enrolls close to one hundred students every fall semester. It features a weekly guest-speaker series that acquaints students with the diverse career paths open to them. But the very first class focused on familiarizing students with their laptops and how to use them. A computer specialist reviewed the software they needed, how to use e-mail, and how to submit their weekly reports as attachments.

The freshmen used their laptops to take notes on the speakers' presentations, write weekly one-page reports, prepare a résumé, and summarize an interview with their faculty academic advisor. (To replace any presentations they missed, we encouraged our freshmen to attend designated AVS

New Directions for Teaching and Learning, no. 101, Spring 2005 © Wiley Periodicals, Inc. 61

graduate seminars. It was not unusual to see our students in these seminars taking notes on their laptops.) Students electronically submitted all their documents except their class notes. This alone helped the faculty tremendously; it cut down on paperwork, ensured that all student work followed a standard format, made it easier to find and mark grammar and spelling errors, and reduced the grading time required.

These first-year students also learned how to stay abreast of the field of animal science. One major team assignment sent students out on the Web to find sources of late-breaking news in the livestock and poultry industries—material missing from the textbook. They then developed reference materials to share with other teams and to archive for future classes.

Animal Sciences Techniques is a hands-on course taught in the second semester of the freshman year. Its fourteen laboratories take students from the beef, equine, and swine farms to the abattoir and taste-testing kitchen. Students learn the basic anatomy and physiology of livestock as well as basic husbandry and livestock management techniques such as injection, castration, tattooing, ear tagging, halter breaking and fitting, and showing of various species.

One assignment in particular lent itself well to laptop use: the behavior project, in which each student was assigned an animal or group of animals to observe unobtrusively for three weeks. In the past, students wrote their behavioral observations on any available scrap of paper. But this year we saw them sitting in the alleyways of the poultry, equine, swine, dairy, and beef farms recording their observations on their laptops. Thanks to this new technology, students lost less information and collected more consistent data for their final reports. When they presented a summary of their observations in their lab section, many elected to give PowerPoint presentations with digital images and graphs on their laptops.

The digital materials that our first-year students developed in these two introductory courses, along with their résumés, became the first contribution to their electronic portfolios. We are preparing these students for their long-term college career, as Clemson University is moving toward requiring all undergraduates to construct two such portfolios to document their learning before graduation.

The Challenges of the Laptop in Animal Sciences

Past the introductory-course level, incorporating laptops into an animal science curriculum presents some unique challenges. Students in the AVS major spend considerable time at the animal farms, at least some of it in the abattoir. They must be able to connect their laptops with the network, record extensive data, and recharge their batteries as needed.

Remote Locations. Much of the learning occurs in hands-on laboratories and other class meetings at the farms, which are really the only place where students can practice livestock management and husbandry. In addition, students conducting foaling and parturition projects must often spend all night at the farm waiting for their mare or cow to deliver an off-spring while taking notes on the timing and physiological changes associated with the birthing process.

Therefore, to integrate laptops throughout our curriculum we need high-speed Internet connections with wireless hubs at eight to ten animal farm locations. Because these farms are located in remote, sparsely populated areas, they are low priority for companies providing digital subscriber lines (DSL) or cable Internet service. Fortunately, however, most of them are reasonably close to the underground fiber-optic cables that link the university's primary computer operations (the mainframe and most of the servers) with the main campus ten miles away. So we have been extending these cables to the various farms. The poultry and diary farms were first in line to get wireless and host laptop courses.

Another push behind our incorporating wireless on the animal farms is the federal Department of Agriculture U.S. Animal Identification Plan (USAIP). This new plan requires each animal to have a unique identifier for tracking in case of a disease outbreak. Of course, these identifiers can be useful for other purposes as well, such as monitoring animals' health and weight gain, recording their vaccinations and parasite treatments, and synchronizing their identification with the weight recorded as they cross the scales. Although use of radio frequency identification (RFID) is not yet standardized in the cattle industry, land-grant universities must take the lead and familiarize students with likely future technologies and their applications in livestock management. At Clemson, we are taking the lead by implementing the university laptop mandate.

Need for Freedom of Movement. Another challenge to using a laptop on an animal farm is the need for hands-free computing as well as overall freedom of movement. A laptop is a relatively large and bulky object to be carrying around while examining good-sized animals and, at the same time, trying to stay out of their way. Both the students and the laptops can be hit hard at any moment.

This issue inspired a group of laptop faculty from AVS and other departments to develop some recommendations on laptop use. The best suggestion solves a number of problems: specific workstations or podiums to securely hold the laptops while students are working with the livestock. These workstations will have electrical outlets, which also solves the power problem. Even the best-planning students need to recharge their batteries at the farm because many of the labs are held late in the day and require two to three hours of laptop use.

Damp, Cold Environments. A third issue we're addressing is the computer-unfriendly environment at the farm and the abattoir conditions, which could shorten the life of a laptop. The farms tend to be dusty and sometimes cold and wet. Covered workstations or podiums will protect the computers from some of these elements.

But the abattoir, with its harshly cold temperature, high humidity, and the constant condensation endemic to coolers and freezers, is another story, one without an affordable solution at the moment. When our freshmen visit the abattoir, we do not require them to bring a laptop. Instead, we make digital pictures of the place available to them after the visit. Fortunately, only a few AVS classes, those dealing with meats and carcass evaluation, spend much time in the abattoir.

Biosecurity. A final potential problem with laptops is the risk of disease transmission, which the movement of people and equipment onto a farm increases. We already take strict precautions. For example, we do not allow onto the farm visitors who have been out of the country, at a livestock auction, or around sick animals during the previous two weeks. In addition, visitors must wear clean coveralls and rubber boots without laces or buckles. Laptops present a very small biohazard risk, but we are considering applying an exterior sanitizer to each laptop case or issuing a disposable sleeve to fit over a laptop.

Specific Applications of Laptops in Major Courses

The three of us AVS laptop faculty represent three distinct commodity groups (dairy cattle, beef cattle, and poultry) and three unique disciples (nutrition, physiology, and management). We have each developed our own specific plans to integrate laptops into our classes.

Physiology and Poultry. Because the poultry farm was equipped with wireless first, coauthor Birrenkott's Poultry and Poultry Products Evaluation course was the first in the AVS major to make full use of laptops. It is a hands-on, lab-based course in which students learn to evaluate chicken carcasses, egg types (broken-out, candled, and exterior), and live chickens for their egg and meat qualities. During each lab, students determined the USDA grade for one hundred or more eggs, carcasses, and live birds, entering their evaluations on the laptop and submitting them electronically. The course management system then performed what used to be the instructor's tedious task of correcting the thousands of individual responses and recording the grades.

Birrenkott will soon have his students using their laptops in his physiology courses (animal, avian, and reproductive) as well. In the labs, students will use them to record and share physiological data (heart and respiratory rates, EKG, muscle twitches, and action potentials). Then they will add these data to those they collected in their first-year AVS courses. At this higher level, however, students will perform more complex statistical data analysis for summation in their laboratory reports. Birrenkott and his colleagues are also developing online tutorials on how to use a variety of laboratory equipment. Students will download and review these tutorials *before* the lab, which will free up instructor time in lab and help ensure that students come to lab prepared.

Birrenkott's physiology courses also introduce students to the microscopic anatomy and physiology of various organ systems, so he is developing a digital-image database that students will access to compare what they are observing through the microscope with comparable labeled images. This innovation will eliminate the need for a bulky histology textbook. An additional benefit is that the large size of the images will facilitate learning for visually impaired students.

Laptops will also allow students to perform the statistical analyses required in some of the lab exercises. For example, in reproductive physiology, students will measure the testosterone levels in anonymous saliva samples, construct standard curves, plot the results, and compare the average level of the hormone in males and females. In another reproduction lab, students dissect bovine placenta from a local abattoir and measure the crown-to-rump length of the fetus. Using laptops, students will be able to estimate fetal age by plotting these measurements against bovine-fetus standards. They will also take detailed notes on morphological and anatomical development.

Livestock Techniques, Production, Breeding, and Evaluation. Co-author Bolt teaches animal techniques, beef and swine production, animal breeding, and livestock evaluation. His two techniques courses cover the basic husbandry of beef cattle and swine. Students will first use laptops to view reference materials and multimedia presentations on the laboratory procedures before the actual lab exercise. They will then collect production data at the farms and apply them in assignments on making management decisions, all on the laptop. Bolt will start out using commercial software simulations with multivariable input fields for making livestock management decisions, but he plans to develop more such simulations using data generated on Clemson's animal farms. He also hopes to create a bulletin board that links his students to both students and faculty at other animal sciences departments to get feedback on their management decisions.

Bertrand, a ruminant nutritionist, teaches the dairy techniques course, in which each student is assigned a cow that will calve during the semester. Two weeks before the cow's due date, students start to visit her every day and are present when she calves. They continue to visit her and her calf twice during the first week after the birth. During these visits, they record their observations in their journal for eventual incorporation into a written in-depth report. Laptops proved to be the perfect journaling and report-writing medium; students were able to copy and paste relevant observations from their journal into their report. They also used their laptop to graph their cow's milk weights after she calved and returned to the milking herd and to calculate her lifetime profit or loss.

Principles of Animal Nutrition relies on a variety of multimedia tools, and laptops will allow students to access these tools in class. In the next course in the sequence, Applied Animal Nutrition, students will use laptops to calculate rations for various types of animals and to determine least-cost diet formulations.

Across the AVS Courses. Much of the AVS knowledge that students in the major must master involves quantitative data collection, calculations, and graphing. Until recently, we assigned spreadsheet and graphing exercises as homework and were unable to help those students struggling with the software. With laptops we had single students or teams do these exercises in class, where we were able to provide more in-depth and individualized instruction. We also added exercises (for example, calculating the profit or loss for the lifetime of an animal) that we couldn't assign before because they would have required holding class in a computer lab.

In the Future

During these early laptop years, students have complained about carrying the added weight of a laptop to class every day and the shortage of wireless hubs and electrical connections in classrooms and study areas. But with each passing year, laptops grow lighter and wireless hubs more numerous. (Electrical connections are a more stubborn challenge.) The faculty have voiced concern about students' inappropriate use of laptops during class (playing games, surfing the Web, instant-messaging, and checking e-mail). But a number of simple solutions are available, among which is occasionally moving behind the students to see if anyone is off-task (Nilson, 2003).

Despite these drawbacks, the AVS faculty and students at Clemson are excited about the new learning opportunities that laptops bring to our undergraduate curriculum. As we continue to overcome the challenges that this technology presents to our discipline, we will expand our ambitious plans for preparing our students for the innovative agricultural technologies of the future.

Reference

Nilson, L. B. *Teaching at Its Best: A Research-Based Resource for College Instructors* (2nd ed.). Bolton, Mass.: Anker, 2003.

GLENN BIRRENKOTT *is professor and coordinator of undergraduate programs in the Department of Animal and Veterinary Sciences at Clemson University.*

JEAN A. BERTRAND *is professor and chair of the curriculum committee of the Department of Animal and Veterinary Sciences at Clemson University.*

BRIAN BOLT *is a lecturer in the Department of Animal and Veterinary Sciences at Clemson University.*

8

Teaching first-year engineering students in a laptop environment requires carefully choosing and then adapting teaching methods. This chapter describes how laptops were used, how the students responded, and what the group of participating faculty learned in the process.

Using Laptops in Engineering Courses for Real-Time Data Collection and Analysis

Matthew W. Ohland, Elizabeth A. Stephan

Although it is commonly assumed that the use of computer technology in the classroom has significant potential to benefit the educational process, evidence supporting the assumption is still modest (Neal, 1998). A growing body of literature on strategic management of technology in higher education asserts that technology is increasingly, inevitably, and ubiquitously a part of education. Katz and Associates (1999) ascribe learning benefits to technology, yet they present no evidence of its benefits to student learning. The Alfred P. Sloan Foundation, which has invested nearly $50 million in the Sloan Program in Anytime, Anyplace Learning, presents highlights of a recent survey focusing mostly on increasing enrollment rather than enhancing student learning (Sloan, 2004). Bates (2000) enumerates "How Technology Is Changing Teaching" yet refers to no studies

Note: This material is based on work supported by NSF award no. 0127052, "Clemson's Experimental Engineering in Real-Time (EXPERT) Program." The authors wish to acknowledge that Benjamin L. Sill and William J. Park contributed significantly to the development of the laboratories and the teaching methods discussed. John Minor's fresh perspective of using the sensors in the classroom helped improve the laboratories. Postdoctoral associate Amy G. Yuhasz managed the design and execution of the educational experiment. Clemson undergraduate students helped develop and test classroom activities: Sunil Bector, Joshua Bloom, Michael Boggs, Jonathan Brown, Curtis Culbreath, Benjamin Eddy, Mark Goettsch, Keith Press, Justin Reeder, Christopher Von Ins, and Alex Wensley. Clemson art majors Kim Dick and Nathan Hadley rendered the laboratory drawings. High school students Jessica Latour and Roy Welsh tested the initial laboratories.

supporting his assertion that new technologies improve the teaching of higher-order learning skills.

Bates and Poole (2003), however, put the issue of educational technology in the proper perspective. They identify the most significant challenge in studying how technology affects learning: the media is typically confounded with the message. Thus, in comparing technology-enhanced learning to traditional methods, it is difficult to design an experiment in which all other things are equal. Bates and Poole also point out (2003) that gaining a better understanding of how technology enhances learning requires that we use it even though the effect is not completely understood.

This chapter focuses on how we used laptops in combination with sensor-based technology and other pedagogical approaches that are known to improve student learning. In the process, we created a classroom environment in which the technology was enabling, creating educational experiences that would not be possible otherwise. Here we present our preliminary results from an ongoing study of student learning.

The Learning Environment: Our Students, Courses, and Classrooms

Clemson University is a rural land-grant institution in upstate South Carolina. It has technical foundations and still maintains a technical focus; the College of Engineering and Science is the largest college of five in the university. The General Engineering Program has coordinated a common first-year engineering curriculum since 1985.

About one in eight of Clemson's General Engineering students has not taken high school physics, 80 percent start the mathematics sequence in Calculus I, and about one in ten is not calculus-ready at matriculation. The average SAT score of first-year students in the College of Engineering and Science is about 1250.

The first-semester course, Introduction to Engineering Disciplines and Skills, enrolls eight hundred mostly first-time-in-college students. It provides detail on the various majors in the college and introduces elementary engineering material, including units, dimensions, estimation, graphs, spreadsheets, and experimentation. This course is a descendant of Introduction to Engineering and Science, which is described in greater detail elsewhere (Ohland and Sill, 2002; Ohland, Sill, and Crockett, 2002). One of the course objectives is to acquaint students with the design process; a variety of design projects have been used to meet this objective (Sill, Ohland, and Stephan, 2003).

The second-semester course, Engineering Fundamentals, offers multiple sections with different disciplinary emphases. It helps students confirm their choice of major and develop skills more specific to their interests. This course is a descendant of Introduction to Engineering Problem Solving and Design, which is described by Sill, Ohland, and Stephan (2003). This course enrolls approximately six hundred students per year, including some transfer students.

In both semesters, students meet each week for a one-hour lecture and a two-hour lab. The lecture typically meets in a large theater-style lecture hall equipped with continuous tables and movable chairs. The labs typically meet in a small-group classroom equipped with oval tables and movable chairs, or in our project lab, which has workbench-style tables and stools. Our entire building is wireless, and the college has required all entering students to have a laptop since 2002. Undergraduate teaching assistants attend class to facilitate instruction and hold evening office hours.

We assign project teams to be of heterogeneous academic ability using predicted grade point ratios computed by the Admissions Office. We try to ensure that women and minorities are not outnumbered on a team (Felder and Brent, 1994).

The Approach to Learning: Desired Pedagogies

Research suggests that exclusive use of the lecture in the classroom constrains students' learning (Bonwell and Eison, 1991), but use of technology does not guarantee improvement. Its effectiveness depends on both the advantages of the technology itself and the ability of the instructor to incorporate it into a busy schedule. The benefits of active learning experiences in the classroom are well documented, notably better attendance, deeper questioning, higher grades, and a lasting interest in the subject matter (Johnson, Johnson, and Smith, 1998; Bonwell and Eison, 1991; Felder, 1992; McKeachie, Pintrich, Lin, and Smith, 1986; Wankat and Oreovicz, 1993). Of particular interest is evidence highlighting the benefits of active and cooperative learning in engineering and science classes (Felder, Felder, and Dietz, 1998; Hake, 1998; Springer, Stanne, and Donovan, 1997; Bowen and Phelps, 1997; Caprio, 1993; Carpenter and McMillan, 2003; Cooper, 1995; Felder, 1996; Kogut, 1997; Mourtos, 1997; Redish and Steinberg, 1999; Rosser, 1999). Another form of active learning is discovery learning; the research finds that it promotes deeper understanding and long-term retention (Travers, 1982). Similarly, learning improves when students are coached but not directed to a solution (Tribus, 1971). Unfortunately, discovery learning has never gained widespread use because of its potential time inefficiencies (Jacobs, 1992).

With the university laptop mandate, we were able to introduce a powerful, discovery-based instructional technology that depends on students using laptops in class. This technology has been well researched. The literature on microcomputer-based learning shows that students demonstrate improved understanding of physical concepts and their graphical representation when electronic sensors are used to gather and display data in real time (Thornton and Sokoloff, 1990; Brasell, 1987; Redish, Saul, and Steinberg, 1997; Beichner, 1996). It is no surprise that seeing graphical output from electronic sensors in real time makes for effective learning; these techniques are discovery-based and active.

To study whether this approach has an educational benefit beyond other active, discovery-based learning, Clemson received a grant from the National Science Foundation (Ohland, Stephan, and Sill, 2003; Ohland, Stephan, Sill, and Park, 2004). While controlling for other learning-related variables, the experimental study compares student performance in sensor-based lab activities to student performance in parallel lab activities that do not use sensors (Yuhasz, Ohland, and Stephan, 2004).

Adapting Proven Pedagogies to the Laptop Classroom

As Bates and Poole (2003) predict, managing this educational experiment has been a challenge. We frequently had to adapt our teaching approach to accommodate the limitations and potentials of the laptop and sensor-based technologies.

Group Size. Prior to the laptop mandate, all faculty in Clemson's Department of General Engineering divided their classes into groups of four for interactive, in-class learning activities. These four-person groupings functioned well in all our teaching settings. In our theater-style lecture hall, movable seats permitted student pairs from adjacent rows to face each other. In our smaller classrooms, four-person tables fostered this same kind of interaction. In our project laboratory, four students shared a workbench.

But the introduction of laptops rendered this configuration unacceptable. If four students in any of those configurations work on a laptop, the student whose laptop is in use and the one on the same side of the table are able to see the laptop, but the other two students see only the back of the laptop. Three students can see a laptop from the same side of a table, *if* the laptop is in front of the center person. In settings with relatively large tables, then, groups of three are acceptable. But in a setting with shorter tables (which describes our laboratory set-up), we hypothesized that students would have to work in pairs on laptops to ensure universal engagement and adequate visibility.

We tested this hypothesis on our 438 General Engineering students at the end of the spring semester of 2004. We surveyed their opinion of the pair arrangement with this agree-disagree item: "When using the sensors, someone else in my group always operated the computer, and I wasn't involved." Fewer than 10 percent of the students agreed with the statement, giving us confidence that the pair arrangement fostered student engagement.

Student Maturity. In a theater setting, General Engineering faculty commonly used active learning techniques suitable to that environment, such as think-pair-share (Lyman, 1987; Kagan, 1994). In this large group setting, our first-year students were significantly distracted by the use of laptops. So we chose to eliminate laptop use in lecture and required students to put their laptops away. However, more mature students, such as those in junior-level computer science classes using the same theater, did make proper use of laptops in the lecture setting.

The Pace of Learning. The use of electronic sensors connected to laptops automated data collection, making many laboratory exercises move more quickly. Unfortunately, this seemed to encourage students to rush through the lab and leave early, jeopardizing their ability to comprehend the data collected and assimilate meaningful conclusions. To slow down the labs a bit and foster deeper processing, we introduced structured reflection.

The reflection process complemented the discovery methods we were using, because both shift some control over the learning process to the learner. The benefits of doing so are well documented by Goforth (1994) in his meta-analysis of the effectiveness of learner control in tutorial computer-assisted instruction. The use of mastery-based activities and self-paced problem solving in a resource-rich environment (with peers, the instructor, and the undergraduate assistant available to help) gives even more control to the student. This approach was particularly useful in allowing students who had already mastered the material through prior experience to demonstrate their mastery in that area.

Positive Interdependence. Automation of data collection in the labs also reduced the workload of the group, leaving some group members idle, distracted, and disengaged. Our initial response was to increase the workload to ensure positive interdependence. But since each student was responsible for understanding the additional material, the heavier workload could not be divided among group members; the workload increased for *all* students. We then faced the additional challenge that some laboratory procedures were either conceptually sequential or required the same equipment for execution, so the laboratory activities could not be conducted in parallel. Ultimately, the reduction in group size discussed earlier restored positive interdependence.

Individual Accountability. Although tests and quizzes accounted for individual mastery of the material, we wanted to encourage students to master the material before leaving class, so that homework could address extensions to the material. We established checkpoints during class activities at which the instructor or an undergraduate teaching assistant examined the material before the student continued in the activity. This approach was particularly useful when teaching computer skills with software such as Excel and Matlab; students worked on solving a problem with the help of other students, the instructor, and undergraduate assistants.

Figures 8.1 and 8.2 illustrate the approach taken in class. Students were given a small table of position-and-time data and asked to produce a properly formatted plot of the position data as a function of time. Figure 8.1 shows a successful result, modified from the default format in Excel (whereas Excel commonly shades the plot frame, the shading has been removed; similarly, since raw data are plotted, the data points are represented by unconnected symbols). Once students created a properly formatted graph of

Figure 8.1. Position Graph Produced During In-Class Exercise

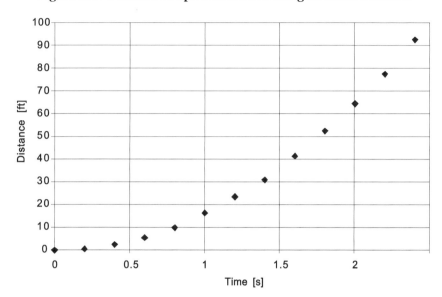

position and time, they needed to calculate and plot a velocity profile; Figure 8.2 shows the resulting profile. The questions accompanying these in-class exercises asked students to struggle with important concepts. In this case, for example, students had to explain why the position curve was smooth but the velocity curve was much less smooth. Their subsequent calculation and graph of acceleration departed even further from the smooth appearance of the position versus time graph. Thus, even though the class activity focused on learning how to use Excel, students discovered the sensitivity of derivative quantities along the way.

Gathering Data from the Internet. On several occasions, students used their laptops to gather Internet data in class, including the values of problem parameters. Students searched reliable sources for physical parameters, background material, and the effect of problem constraints.

Sharing and Integrating Data. Students performed several experiments that required sensors and laptops to collect and analyze the data. Examples of these lab exercises are studying vibration (Figure 8.3) and pH response (Figure 8.4), which happen too quickly for manual data collection, and collecting relational data of force versus displacement (Figure 8.5) or voltage versus current on the same time baseline. With the data in electronic form, we had student groups share their data with other groups so they could compile a more complete data set and acquire a fuller, more accurate understanding of the phenomenon. Figure 8.6 shows a summary of data collected by various groups investigating how the time at which

Figure 8.2. Velocity Graph Produced During In-Class Exercise

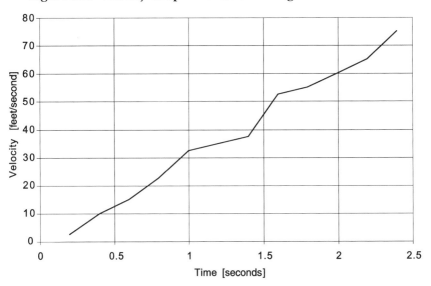

creamer is added to coffee affects the time it takes for the coffee to reach a drinkable temperature.

Efficient Use of Equipment. Placing students in pairs for lab activities as opposed to a larger group required an additional investment in the real-time sensors that attached to student laptops. In fact, switching from four-person groups to pairs required *twice* as many sensors; double this figure *again* if the laboratories of two course sections are scheduled simultaneously. We managed the high cost of the smaller groups by diversifying the lab activities and rotating students through stations around the room.

Diversification required that the day's activities use different sensors and be independent as to their order of completion. In this way, all students in the class could conduct the same activities. In a modified version of the arrangement, groups completed different activities, which worked well when we allowed groups to select from a set of activities typical to various disciplines. This approach also lent itself well to the "jigsaw" method of teaching, in which various students or groups of students construct partial knowledge and then teach each other what they have learned to complete their knowledge (Aronson and others, 1978; Johnson, Johnson, and Smith, 1998).

Our other strategy was establishing stations around our laboratory with the real-time sensors already attached to the equipment. Here we took advantage of the portability of the laptop. Student groups proceeded around

Figure 8.3. Measuring Vibration of a Ruler Using a Motion Sensor

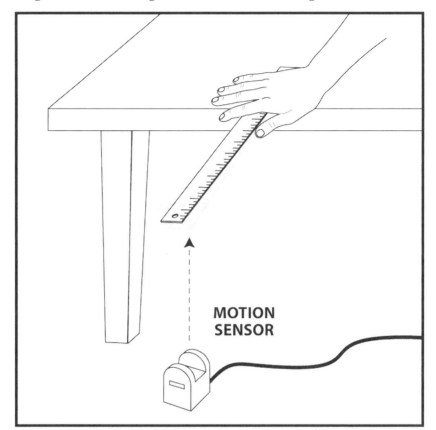

the room to visit each station, sequentially if necessary. In addition, this approach saved set-up time and reduced the cost of auxiliary equipment needed for conducting activities.

Establishing an Environment for Success in a Laptop Classroom

We made varied adjustments to the classroom to support both classroom management and cooperative learning, such as installing movable seating (even in our theater space). To help students get their laptops ready for classroom use and keep them that way, we developed a handout of frequently asked questions (FAQs) with solutions to problems students commonly encountered. An early mastery-based assignment ensured that all students had properly installed software on their laptops. We assessed students a grade penalty for not bringing a working laptop to class unless

Figure 8.4. Fast Response Times of pH Measurement Prohibiting Manual Measurement

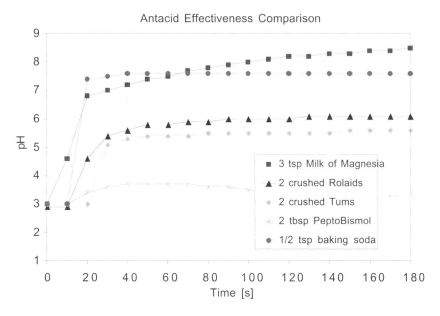

Figure 8.5. Measuring Force and Displacement of a Spring Simultaneously

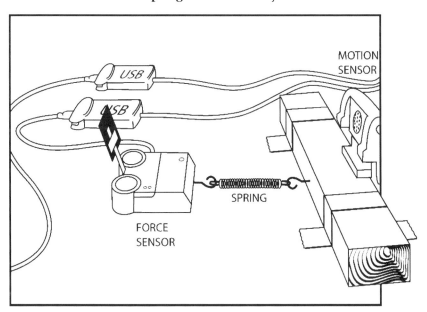

Figure 8.6. Data Collected by Student Groups Investigating Coffee Cooling to Drinkable Temperature (When Creamer Should Be Added)

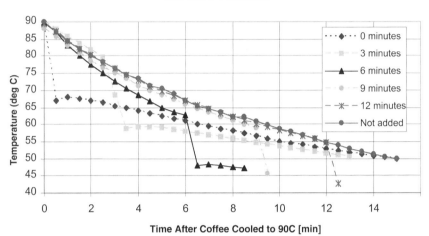

they presented a written excuse for laptop repair from the campus computer facility.

We were forced to make certain adjustments to our teaching because of technological difficulties we experienced. DataStudio, the software that collects data from the Pasco PasPort sensors we used, conflicted with certain spyware programs, so we taught students how to remove them. Personal online activities such as instant messaging interrupted real-time data collection, so we forbade use of such programs in class. We also struggled with overloading the wireless network with network-intensive processes, the worst of these being network installation of software such as DataStudio and particularly Matlab. So we require students to install these applications prior to class for part of their in-class grade. We even struggled as a number of students attempted to connect to another wireless network service, a commercial operator in downtown Clemson.

Summarizing Our Experience with Laptops in the Classroom

Our experience using laptops in the classroom, particularly in conjunction with real-time sensors, helped us understand how to manage in-class use of the technology and adapt cooperative learning and other teaching methods to it. We also learned how to enable students to take advantage of the unique features of the medium. We gave students the opportunity to collect and process data, learn visually by generating and displaying graphs and diagrams, gather and review information in varied locations, research information on the Internet, and share and integrate experimental findings to gain a fuller and clearer understanding of physical phenomena.

We were particularly pleased with the ingenious problem-solving approaches we saw some students initiate, so pleased that we started awarding prizes for original thinking in class activities. For example, one student pair made innovative use of the laptop-sensor combination in an outdoor lab exercise where the technology was not required. The object of the exercise was to determine the velocity of a rubber chicken (a simulation of the University of South Carolina Gamecock mascot) launched by a large slingshot. The standard equipment was usually a radar gun. But the innovative pair used two synchronized motion sensors to measure the time it took the chicken to pass those two points. From this time measurement, the students easily calculated the velocity of the chicken; they obtained an answer comparable to that given by the radar gun.

Although we could observe only the increase in student creativity, we were able to survey student opinions of the technology and the learning benefits they perceived. In our end-of-spring-semester survey, 44 percent of our 438 students agreed with the statement "When using the sensors, it was exciting to manipulate a process variable and see its immediate effect on the graph output of other process variables." In addition, 60 percent agreed with "Using the sensors helped me learn to interpret graphs"; 59 percent agreed that "Using the sensors improved my ability to predict the appearance of a graph."

In view of positive student reactions like these, we plan to continue teaching General Engineering with the winning combination of student laptops and real-time motion sensors. We also expect to refine and expand our use of the technology and extend our research on its effects on student learning.

References

Aronson, E., Blaney, N., Stephin, C., Sikes, J., and Snapp, M. *The Jigsaw Classroom.* Thousand Oaks, Calif.: Sage, 1978.

Bates, A. W. *Managing Technological Change: Strategies for College and University Leaders.* San Francisco: Jossey-Bass, 2000.

Bates, A. W., and Poole, G. *Effective Teaching with Technology in Higher Education: Foundations for Success.* San Francisco: Jossey-Bass, 2003.

Beichner, R. J. "The Impact of Video Motion Analysis on Kinematics Graph Interpretation Skills." *American Journal of Physics,* 1996, 64(10), 1272–1277.

Bonwell, C., and Eison, J. *Active Learning: Creating Excitement in the Classroom.* ASHE-ERIC Higher Education Report no. 1. Washington, D.C.: School of Education and Human Development, George Washington University, 1991.

Bowen, C. W., and Phelps, A. J. "Demonstration-Based Cooperative Testing in General Chemistry: A Broader Assessment-of-Learning Technique." *Journal of Chemical Education,* 1997, 74, 715–719.

Brasell, H. "The Effect of Real-Time Laboratory Graphing on Learning Graphic Representations of Distance and Velocity." *Journal of Research in Science Teaching,* 1987, 24(4), 385–395.

Caprio, M. "Cooperative Learning: The Crown Jewel Among Motivational-Teaching Techniques." *Journal of College Science Teaching,* 1993, *22*(5), 279–281.

Carpenter, S. R., and McMillan, T. "Incorporation of a Cooperative Learning Technique in Organic Chemistry." *Journal of Chemical Education,* 2003, *80,* 330–331.

Cooper, M. "Cooperative Learning: An Approach for Large Enrollment Courses." *Journal of Chemical Education,* 1995, *72,* 162–164.

Felder, R. M. "How About a Quick One." In "Random Thoughts" (feature). *Chemical Engineering Education,* 1992, *26*(1), 18–19.

Felder, R. M. "Active-Inductive-Cooperative Learning: An Instructional Model for Chemistry?" *Journal of Chemical Education,* 1996, *73,* 832–836.

Felder, R. M., and Brent, R. "Cooperative Learning in Technical Courses: Procedures, Pitfalls, and Payoffs." Washington, D.C.: ERIC Document Reproduction Service, 1994. (ED 377 038)

Felder, R. M., Felder, G. N., and Dietz, E. J. "A Longitudinal Study of Engineering Student Performance and Retention. V. Comparisons with Traditionally Taught Students." *Journal of Engineering Education,* 1998, *98*(4), 469–480.

Goforth, D. "Learner Control = Decision Making + Information: A Model and Meta-Analysis." *Journal of Educational Computing Research,* 1994, *11*(1), 1–26.

Hake, R. R. "Interactive Engagement vs. Traditional Methods: A Six-Thousand-Student Survey of Mechanics Test Data for Introductory Physics Courses." *American Journal of Physics,* 1998, *66,* 64–74.

Jacobs, G. "Hypermedia and Discovery-Based Learning: A Historical Perspective." *British Journal of Educational Technology,* 1992, *23*(2), 113–121.

Johnson, D. W., Johnson, R. T., and Smith, K. *Active Learning: Cooperation in the College Classroom.* Edina, N.M.: Interaction Book, 1998.

Kagan, S. *Cooperative Learning.* San Juan Capistrano, Calif.: Kagan's Cooperative Learning, 1994.

Katz, R. N., and Associates. *Dancing with the Devil: Information Technology and the New Competition in Higher Education.* San Francisco: Jossey-Bass, 1999.

Kogut, K. L. "Using Cooperative Learning to Enhance Performance in General Chemistry." *Journal of Chemical Education,* 1997, *74,* 720–722.

Lyman, F. "Think-Pair-Share: An Expanding Teaching Technique." *MAA-CIE Cooperative News,* 1987, *1,* 1–2.

McKeachie, W. J., Pintrich, P., Lin, Y., and Smith, D. *Teaching and Learning in the College Classroom: A Review of the Research Literature, 1986.* Ann Arbor: Regents of University of Michigan, 1986.

Mourtos, N. J. "The Nuts and Bolts of Cooperative Learning in Engineering." *Journal of Engineering Education,* 1997, *86,* 35–37.

Neal, E. "We Need to Exercise Healthy Skepticism." *Chronicle of Higher Education,* June 19, 1998, p. B4.

Ohland, M. W., and Sill, B. L. "Demonstrating the Added Value of an Introduction to Engineering Course." *Proceedings, 2002 Frontiers in Education Conference,* Boston, 2002.

Ohland, M. W., Sill, B. L., and Crockett, E. R. "Thinking About the Scheduling of the Introduction to Engineering Syllabus: Using a Just-in-Time Approach." *Proceedings, 2002 American Society of Engineering Education Conference,* Montreal, Quebec, Canada, 2002.

Ohland, M. W., Stephan, E. A., and Sill, B. L. "Clemson University's EXPerimental Engineering in Real Time (EXPERT) Program: Assessing the Benefit of Real-Time Sensors in the Curriculum." *Proceedings, 2003 American Society of Engineering Education Conference,* Nashville, Tenn., 2003.

Ohland, M. W., Stephan, E. A., Sill, B. L., and Park, W. J. "Applications of Real-Time Sensors in the Freshman Engineering Classroom." *Proceedings, 2004 American Society of Engineering Education Conference,* Salt Lake City, Utah, 2004.

Redish, E. F., and Steinberg, R. N. "Teaching Physics: Figuring Out What Works." *Physics Today*, Jan. 1999, pp. 24–30.

Redish, E. F., Saul, J. M., and Steinberg, R. N. "On the Effectiveness of Active-Engagement Microcomputer-Based Laboratories." *American Journal of Physics*, 1997, 65, 45–54.

Rosser, S. V. "Group Work in Science, Engineering, and Mathematics." *College Teaching*, 1999, 46(3), 82–88.

Sill, B. L., Ohland, M. W., and Stephan, E. A. "Keeping the 'General' in General Engineering: Designing Multidisciplinary Courses for the First Year of Engineering." *Proceedings, 2003 American Society of Engineering Education Conference*, Nashville, Tenn., 2003.

Sloan Foundation. "Sloan Program in Anytime, Anyplace Learning: History and Additional Details for 2004 Directions," 2004. Retrieved July 30, 2004, from http://www.sloan.org/programs/historystatus.shtml.

Springer, L., Stanne, M. E., and Donovan, S. S. *Effects of Small-Group Learning on Undergraduates in Science, Mathematics, Engineering, and Technology: A Meta-Analysis.* Research Monograph no. 11. Madison, Wis.: National Institute for Science Education, 1997.

Thornton, R. K., and Sokoloff, D. R. "Learning Motion Concepts Using Real-Time Microcomputer-Based Laboratory Tools." *American Journal of Physics*, 1990, 58(9), 858–867.

Travers, R. M. *Essentials of Learning: The New Cognitive Learning for Students of Education* (5th ed.). New York: Macmillan, 1982.

Tribus, M. "Education for Innovation." *Engineering Education*, Feb. 1971, p. 421.

Wankat, P., and Oreovicz, F. *Teaching Engineering.* New York: McGraw-Hill, 1993.

Yuhasz, A. G., Ohland, M. W., and Stephan, E. A. "The Use of Sensors in the Engineering Classroom: Experimental Design Considerations." *Proceedings, 2004 American Society of Engineering Education Conference*, Salt Lake City, Utah, 2004.

MATTHEW W. OHLAND *is assistant professor in the General Engineering Program at Clemson University and president of Tau Beta Pi, the national engineering honor society.*

ELIZABETH A. STEPHAN *is an instructor in the General Engineering Program at Clemson University.*

9

This chapter describes successful assignments that made creative use of laptops in writing, literature, and public speaking courses. Some activities moved the session out of the classroom to outdoor locations.

Laptops in the Humanities: Classroom Walls Come Tumbling Down

Barbara E. Weaver

When Clemson University's College of Engineering and Science began its pilot laptop program in 1998, the organizers made a courteous nod to Communication Across the Curriculum by selecting a few English faculty to participate. The success of the English courses surprised faculty from the technical disciplines, who didn't expect laptops to make much difference in the humanities. What the laptops did was increase opportunities for and forms of communication, bring mobility to other physical and virtual places, open the door to more innovative assignments, and fully engage students who professed to hate English. More recently, I have found the same success in teaching public speaking. For my students and me, the classroom walls came tumbling down.

Composition I

The first laptop course I taught was Composition I in fall 1998. I began brainstorming ideas for laptop assignments with two other laptop faculty members, William Park in general engineering and Bernadette Longo in English. We met regularly to share ideas and offer support to one another as we prepared to embark on this new journey. We were excited but we also had reservations. We believed we would successfully integrate laptops into our classes, but we also knew the potential for failure was present. Although not every assignment I made that first semester or since has worked exactly the way I planned, many were successful.

New Directions for Teaching and Learning, no. 101, Spring 2005   © Wiley Periodicals, Inc.   81

Nature and Technology in the South Carolina Botanical Garden.
One of the most successful assignments in first-year composition was an assignment I gave to the students for the second day of class. The concept I wanted to teach was perspective. But I also had other goals in mind that I wanted to incorporate: for students to experience Clemson in a way that was unlikely to be how they had already experienced it on their own, to discover nature and how their work in technical disciplines affects nature, to hone their observation and writing skills, and to effectively and efficiently use computing services at Clemson.

I had the students form teams of four, and together we rode the Clemson Area Transit to the South Carolina Botanical Garden. Each team had to agree on one place where technology and nature collide; then each student on the team chose his or her own perspective. From this individual vantage point, the students recorded their observations on their laptops and took a photo of their perspective. They also took photos of one another sitting in their positions and using their laptops. The next class period, back in the classroom, each individual wrote a descriptive essay based on his or her observations. After reviews and revisions, the students posted their essays and photos to their individual Web pages and then made links to their teammates' pages.

We all enjoyed seeing these clearly illustrated examples of how four people with the same goal can look at the same thing and see something different. One member of a team had a spider drop onto his keyboard, but of course none of his teammates saw the spider. On another team, one student saw a lizard run into the site the team had chosen, though the other team members did not see it. Every student realized that others have their own perspectives. We used this experience to discuss the importance of others' perspectives. As we progressed through the semester and undertook various team assignments, minority students more assertively voiced their perspectives; nonminority students more actively sought minority perspectives and were more willing to really listen to those perspectives. Students even appreciated learning how to ride the transit system and finding a quiet place to study (the Garden). They reported that this was their favorite assignment because by the first week they knew three people in the class, were familiar with their laptops, knew how to make Web pages, and learned an important lesson about perspective they could apply in all their classes in which team projects were assigned.

"Kew Gardens" by Virginia Woolf. For another successful first-year composition assignment, the students used the 1928 edition of the short story "Kew Gardens," by Virginia Woolf, and one of their texts, *Visual Communication: A Writer's Guide,* by Susan Hilligoss. After reading "Kew Gardens," the students complained that the story had no plot, that it was not a real story. They did not understand what Woolf was saying or why she wrote the story. To help them begin to understand the story, we visited the South Carolina Botanical Garden to observe the activity in a garden and try to identify with Woolf. Students captured their observations on their laptops and in digital and print photos. As we left the garden, several students reported, "I get it now."

The next part of the assignment took place in the classroom. First the students formed teams of three. Using the Hilligoss text as their guide, each team evaluated Vanessa Bell's illustrations in the 1928 edition of "Kew Gardens." They posted their evaluations to our course management system and then orally presented their evaluations. After fully discussing their experience in the garden and Bell's illustrations, I asked the students to select a portion of text (any length) from the story and, using the Hilligoss text to guide them, create a digital page with that text. I purposefully did not give them an example to follow or much direction. I wanted them to develop their own insights and how to express those insights digitally. The last part of the assignment was to write a process-and-purpose essay, which explained their process for developing the new page of "Kew Gardens" and articulated their reasons for each decision they made, citing Hilligoss at least twice.

Their results were remarkable, some of such high quality that my words of praise were entirely inadequate. The freedom I gave them to create and the combination of laptop convenience and software unleashed their talents and motivation. One student used Adobe Photoshop to layer his selected text, two photos he took in the garden, and a graphic of a dragonfly from the Internet with an added shadow he created. His digital page and accompanying essay made clear he had internalized "Kew Gardens" to discover its nuance of meaning in his life. By the time the students finished this assignment, they all reported that they truly understood Woolf's purpose in writing the story and that they would always remember the portion of text that it turned out held personal meaning for them.

Habitat for Humanity Homecoming Build. Every Homecoming, Clemson University students build a home for a neighbor in need of a decent place to live. The house is built on campus and moved to its permanent location on the Monday following Homecoming. In fall 1998, Habitat for Humanity advisor Chris Heavner came to my first-year composition classes to tell the students about the student chapter and the Homecoming Build. He explained his need for three PowerPoint presentations: one he could use to solicit funds from major donors, one he could use for a presentation at the Kellogg Regional Conference, and one he could run on a laptop inside the house during Homecoming Weekend.

On the basis of the information they received from Heavner and their own research, the students worked in teams to create the three PowerPoint presentations. They spent one class period helping build the house so they would have a better understanding of their topic, see teamwork illustrated in a community environment, and feel a part of this wonderful Clemson tradition.

They used their laptops in class to develop, review (with Heavner participating in the review), and revise their presentations in class. An unexpected result of the assignment was a new logo for the Homecoming Build at Clemson. Student Jeff Moreland created the logo by combining the Clemson Tiger Paw with the Habitat logo so his team would have an appropriate graphic in their PowerPoint. This led to an additional learning opportunity because the students had to obtain permission from Clemson University's athletic department to use the Tiger Paw. The permission they obtained covers use of the logo for all work associated with all Habitat houses that Clemson students build.

In addition to their PowerPoint presentations, students wrote and produced public service announcements that encouraged community financial contributions; they aired on a local radio station during the week before Homecoming. Students reported that they learned a lot about registered trademarks and copyright law, writing for various media, and working for a client. They also enjoyed the opportunity to contribute to the community.

***Cloud 9* by Caryl Churchill.** This assignment involved students from three laptop sections of Composition I: one taught by Elisa Sparks and two taught by me. We formed teams across sections with the expectation that students would work together primarily online via the course management system. The students' assignment was to design and develop a thorough Web site on the play, which was performed at Clemson University's Brooks Center during fall semester 1999. The play is difficult to understand, and nearly all students in first-year composition had assignments based on the play. The Web site, entitled "Engineering a Play," was used by other instructors (primarily graduate teaching assistants) and their students to help everyone grasp how a play is engineered and understand the content of this particular play.

The thirteen teams focused on backstage, set design, lighting design, sound and music, Churchill and play context, costumes, actors, director, smart things students have said about the play, censorship and reception of the play, rehearsals, basic building blocks of the play (plot, character, and theme), and Web masters.

The students used e-mail to communicate with team members in other sections and their resource contacts, such as Mark Charney, the director of the play. They used the course management system to share files. Peripherals that the students used were digital cameras (taking photos of the actors, the stage, props, lighting, and rehearsals) and scanners to put the costume designs online. Students successfully completed the Web site and learned a lot, but we had a difficult time managing and grading the project. Students complained that Sparks and I did not always give the same answers to questions and that conflicts arose between team members from different instructors' sections. A project of this type is certainly not for the faint of heart. I might try cross-section projects again, but if another instructor is involved I will split the project up differently so each team's members have the same instructor; only then can they hear the same message and be graded by just their own instructor.

Electronic Portfolios. I began assigning e-portfolios in spring 1997, before I had the luxury of having laptops in class. That fall, converting the assignment to a laptop assignment to be worked on in class was easy. The e-portfolios are due at the time of the final exam. Students give me the URL for their online e-portfolio published on their Clemson University homepages and a CD of the files to aid my grading. The portfolio documents the student's academic achievements (not just English), employment, volunteer work, and extracurricular activities. Reflections on student achievements, what they have learned, how they have matured, and their goals are important elements of the e-portfolios. Students reported that they were surprised to discover how much they had accomplished, learned, and matured in such a short time. I noticed, and they reported, an increase in self-esteem in their reflections.

Composition II

Building on the success of my laptop sections of Composition I, I prepared laptop assignments for my spring semester classes of Composition II. Most of the assignments made typical use of the laptops in class to write, review, and revise research papers and submit them by way of the course management system. However, one assignment was new and particularly successful.

The South Carolina Botanical Garden Nature-Based Sculpture Program is a unique opportunity for Clemson University students to work with a visiting artist to help install a nature-based sculpture in the garden. Each year, an artist is invited to spend the month of February designing and installing a nature-based sculpture. To date, twelve artists have installed these ephemeral nature-based sculptures in the garden. My Composition II students attended lectures by visiting artist Karen McCoy; interviewed her, the garden's cultural programs director Ernie Denny, and landscape architecture professor Frances Chamberlain; researched rammed-earth techniques and local history that McCoy requested; worked alongside McCoy to help install the sculpture, documenting their observations in a journal and digital photographs; and completed a writing assignment about their experience.

The writing assignment involved reading and evaluating their hometown newspaper for one month, determining where they might be able to publish an article on the sculpture program in the newspaper, contacting the editor of the paper to arrange publication of the article (or a letter to the editor), writing the article or letter, submitting the article (some with photos) or letter to the newspaper, and submitting the published article or letter to me for additional points. In a class of twenty students, fourteen were successful in getting their work published. Newspapers in Michigan, New York, Pennsylvania, North Carolina, Georgia, and South Carolina ran student-written articles in the Lifestyle or Travel sections or letters to the editor. Several included photographs; one article ran on the front page of the Lifestyle section with two color photographs. The convenience and efficiency of the laptop in recording and storing information and for necessary communication, in addition to writing the article, made this laptop assignment a success for my students.

Contemporary Literature

In my contemporary literature classes, I used the laptops in conjunction with the course management system in some common ways: daily online reading quizzes, essay submission, grading, and so on. But I also developed several assignments beyond those standard uses, one of which—poetry projects—was quite successful in terms of content retention and fun.

To begin the poetry section of the course, we watched a 1987 documentary, *The Beat Generation,* hosted by Steve Allen and directed and produced by Janet Forman. After some discussion, the students grouped themselves into pairs and selected a Beat poet on which to focus. Their goal was to develop an informative and entertaining evening on the Beat poets in collaboration with Linda Dzuris's carillon students. As a class, the students chose the title for their event: "All Along the Bell Tower: An Evening of Carillon and Poetry." In class, the pairs researched their selected poet, developed a PowerPoint presentation, reviewed one another's presentations, and made necessary revisions. They also decided as a class the order of the presentations and planned the attire and refreshments to emulate a coffee house of the Beat Generation.

With all of us dressed in black, wearing sunglasses, and some wearing berets, the event began at dusk with the carillon students' concert in the Tillman Hall bell tower. Below in the amphitheater, my students prepared for their presentations. When darkness fell, my students presented the results of their research. Projecting their combined PowerPoint work on a large screen, they provided a brief biographical sketch of the poet and read at least one poem that they then analyzed. Passersby stopped to have coffee and listen to the presentations. Recently I talked to some of the students in that class; without exception, they tell me all about the poet they presented and the Beat Generation in general.

Public Speaking

After teaching composition and literature laptop courses for two years, I was asked to teach a laptop section of public speaking. I have found that using laptops daily in public speaking is much more difficult than in the writing and literature courses I taught. For starters, when students are giving presentations or a speech they need the undivided attention of their peers. Laptops have proven to be a nuisance on those days, and I have to tell students to shut their laptops unless they are assigned to critique the peer speaker. Every speaker is critiqued by four peers: two thoughtfully complete an online evaluation form, and two give immediate oral comments (two things the speaker did well and two things the speaker needs to improve). Only those four students may use their laptop to take observational notes. I find having to enforce this classroom policy embarrassing (Why will they not pay courteous attention to their peers?) but unfortunately necessary. Three laptop assignments in public speaking merit some explanation.

What Did I Do Wrong? What Should I Have Done Instead? This in-class assignment is fairly simple. Before class begins, I set up my laptop with cords stretched across the room, a microphone that works, and a PowerPoint presentation projected onto a screen at the front of the room. When class begins, I assign the students to one of three elements in public speaking: delivery, content, or audiovisual aids. The students prepare to compose a bulletin board message in the course management system. Then I give the lousiest presentation anyone has ever seen. I trip over the cords, tap on and blow into the microphone, lean on the podium, talk with my back to the students, skip slides, entirely botch the content, and so on. The entire time I am presenting, the students write in their individual bulletin board messages the things I am doing wrong for their assigned area. When I finish presenting, they post their messages. I then pull up a message and we discuss what the student has noted and what I should have done instead. The students thoroughly enjoy this assignment because my presentation is so positively awful that it is funny. But they get the point and do not make the same mistakes themselves.

Botanical Garden Nature-Based Sculpture Program. Not wanting to completely abandon my successful work with writing students and the Garden's sculpture program, I designed a six-week project based on the February event for spring semester public speaking students. As my writing students did, the public speaking students attended the visiting artists' lectures, interviewed the artists, worked alongside the artists to help install the sculpture, and documented their observations in a journal and digital photographs. They researched visiting artists Patrick Dougherty and Yolanda Gutierrez on the Internet and shared their findings with the class. They were then assigned to teams with the goal of designing and developing a multimedia presentation for local elementary school children. Their presentation had to include a brief biographical sketch of the artist, some previous installations, the South Carolina Botanical Garden installation, and a hands-on activity based on a technique used by the artist.

Every team from both classes voiced genuine concern about their ability to capture and maintain the interest of their young audiences. They communicated via e-mail with the teachers of the classes to learn more about their audiences and shared the information with their classmates using the course management system. In class, they prepared, practiced, and revised their presentations. I attended every presentation so I could grade them, and a graduate assistant who works for the Laptop Faculty Development Program digitally recorded their presentations. With no exceptions, my students reported that they learned more from this assignment than they ever would have from in-class speeches to their peers. They also enjoyed presenting to the young children, and some students asked if they could present to a second class.

Electronic Portfolios. Figuring out how to successfully implement an e-portfolio assignment in my public speaking classes was difficult. The first semester I assigned the e-portfolio, I had access to a digital video recorder. At first, I thought it would be easy and wonderful and no trouble at all. But I soon learned that the tape had to be downloaded to a computer and then converted into individual movie files, which took hours. Then students had trouble downloading the large files from the course management system, so I had to burn them onto CDs and pass them around the room. Their finished products were quite good, but I was not convinced it was worth the hours of work and frustration.

Recently, I tried again with a digital recorder that uses DVDs. Again, I was hopeful. But I learned that the conversion process was still necessary. Having no graduate assistant with time to help me, I gave up having the movie files included in their e-portfolios. The students had only their outlines, critiques, and annotated bibliographies to represent their speeches and presentations. The results were lackluster. As technology progresses at Clemson University, e-portfolios that include at least a short clip of a student's best presentation or speech should be possible without requiring an inordinate amount of faculty time.

Conclusion

Through my teaching of laptop courses for eight semesters, I have learned to focus first on my course objectives and ask myself how I can best help students achieve the learning objective. Once I have my vision, I can explore the possibilities of making the vision real through laptops and other technology. What I appreciate most about laptops is the mobility they allow. Some days the best place to be is in the classroom, where wired connections mean quick access to download needed files or visit a virtual place, or where we can close the door for privacy when students need to pay quiet attention to their work. But at other times, the garden, the amphitheater, a local elementary school, or the middle of Bowman Field—where a house is being built by students—is where we need to be. No matter where we meet, students have their work on their laptops and can continue to produce. Classroom walls no longer confine us, but they remain there when we want or need them.

Barbara E. Weaver *manages Clemson University's Laptop Faculty Development Program.*

10

A pioneering administrator of a campus laptop mandate, the author explains how increasingly sophisticated computer enhancements of the curriculum create more and more learning possibilities and potential, with universal laptop ownership in a wireless environment approaching the fullest use of the available technology.

Concluding Comments: Laptop Learning Communities

David G. Brown

The tools available, as well as those *not* available, to learners—for example, textbooks, libraries, laboratories, and classrooms—necessarily shape how faculty teach and students learn. When several students study the same subject at the same time (as in a traditional class), speak the same language, convene regularly in the same classroom, and have convenient access to library materials and laboratories, the professor-leader has a broad range of choices about how to help students learn, about how to structure the course.

If all students own similarly configured laptop computers and have twenty-four-seven access to the Internet, the pedagogical options increase by another order of magnitude. Suddenly, one is free to use digital resources, expect new forms of teamwork among students, depend upon timely communication, involve adjunct professors without regard to geography, manage the course more efficiently, and customize the learning experience for each student. It is no longer necessary to dumb down the curriculum; constrain expectations about when and how students can collaborate; or herd all the students into the same learning sequences, styles, and strategies.

With universal laptop computing, however, comes an awesome responsibility: the responsibility of choice. As professors, each of us must ask anew how the availability of this new resource should change our approach to teaching and learning. Which among the thousands of new alternatives should be pursued? From our previous experience, which strategies have been most effective, and how can laptop computers be used to enhance those strategies?

NEW DIRECTIONS FOR TEACHING AND LEARNING, no. 101, Spring 2005 © Wiley Periodicals, Inc.

Help in meeting this responsibility comes in this valuable volume from Clemson. We learn why faculty teaching in a laptop environment have chosen to use specific methods. We learn about specific techniques.

At Clemson, laptop computers are giving students the chance to collect and analyze data during class, with professorial consultation always accessible. They allow students to assemble at a single location, often during class, to collaborate on team assignments. They facilitate data collection and analysis at sites remote from both the classroom and the dorm.

Student learning has become much, much more active. Music appreciation students are working in teams to analyze components of a CD. Computer science students are replicating professorial demonstrations on their own computers. In sociology, students are seeking out and evaluating alternative approaches to a single subject. Psychology students are blurring the distinction between lab and lecture by becoming actively involved with their own team experiments. Even before class, students in statistics are asking and answering each other's questions. Animal science students are collecting and analyzing data in the real-world settings that they will encounter upon graduation.

Many of us who teach in similar environments will choose to duplicate these strategies. Many others will build upon the strategies in ways more appropriate for their own students, subject matter, personal capacity, and institution. All of us are catalyzed to think more deeply about why and how we teach.

A Spectrum of Possibilities

An environment in which all students have commonly configured laptop computers is well along the spectrum of computer-enhanced campuses. Envision with me a theoretical environment where 100 percent of the learning enhancement potentially achievable from the computer can be realized. What would the defining characteristics of the environment be? Each of us can speculate. Let us start at the bottom.

First, *only some students have computers.* Let us say that some students bring the computers they own to college, and some are able to access a limited number of computers in college-owned laboratories that are open some of the time. Then, most likely, only about 5 percent of the potential improvement in the learning environment can be achieved. The professor cannot equitably expect students to use the learning tools that computers provide.

Second, *all* students have access to a *computer lab.* When all students have twenty-four-seven access to a college-run laboratory, perhaps another 15 percent of the potential can be realized. Equity of access is achieved, and specialized exercises can be assigned for completion between classes. A total of 20 percent of the potential is realizable.

Third, all students have *anytime access to their own computers.* The big change in the potential of the learning environment comes when all students own computers that measure up to a common threshold. The realizable potential jumps from 20 percent to 80 percent. It can now be assumed that all students will check their e-mail at least daily. Specialized communications can be established with subgroups of students. Communication can now occur between professors and students, and among students, at any time. The cycle time in communication between professor and student is shortened. Feedback and collaboration between classes becomes routine.

Fourth, all students *own laptops*. If the commonly owned computers are laptops, another 15 percent of the potential is realized, bringing the total to 95 percent. Now students can team more easily because they can all carry their computers to a "cluster meeting" at a common location. Work can continue over holidays when students are away from campus. Students can carry their computers along to study abroad. Computers can be used in the classroom.

Fifth, all laptops are *wireless on a wireless campus*. The addition of a wireless capacity adds another 3 percent to the potential. Computers can be used at field sites. Connections are likely to be more frequent. Clusters can work anyplace, anytime. All classrooms become "fully Internet accessible."

Sixth, the final increment of potential: the difference between 98 percent potential and 100 percent is accessed by *special-purpose computers*, such as handhelds and tablets. This target is constantly moving as the technology develops.

The overall point to be emphasized is that the laptop environment furnishes fully 95 percent of the potential, and it is probably the most cost-effective way (at least at this time) to take advantage of the information revolution.

What We Know About Learning and About Laptop Computing

The jury is in! First, students learn more quickly, more deeply, and more permanently when they are able to interact with the subject matter, their professor, and student colleagues. The best learning strategies are interactive!

Second, students learn more quickly, more deeply, and more permanently when they help other students learn and are helped along by other students. The best learning strategies are collaborative.

Third, students learn more quickly, more deeply, and more permanently when they are given various ways to learn, when they can approach the same material by reading or by listening or by viewing (and especially by all of the above), when they can hear a lecture multiple times and reread the textbook and redo the experiment. The best learning strategies are multifaceted, multisensory, individualized, and customized.

In summary, the best learning strategies are interactive, collaborative, and customized.

Courses that are computer-enhanced demonstrably involve more interaction and more teamwork, and they offer more numerous multimedia alternatives to learn the material. More powerful than the telephone, more indexable and archivable than face-to-face conversation, and often more inclusive, communication through the Internet is the new powerful learning tool.

Like a cell-phone community, a true community facilitated by the Internet can exist only if all members have a computer and their computers are available in all learning environments. This is the magic of universal laptop programs.

Two Typologies Inspire Course Redesign

The challenge to each professor, new and old, is how to efficiently convert the potential of computers into a real increase in learning. In the laptop environment, new protocols must be imagined, piloted, shared, improved, evaluated, updated, revised, and reimagined.

Whether reshaping a course, redesigning a curriculum, or revising a learning module, one is wisely inspired by specific examples of what "early adopters" have tried. It is likely that a few of these protocols can, with modification, be useful in other courses and other settings. It behooves professors who are redesigning their courses to take fuller advantage of the laptop environment to look first at what others are doing.

In this context, the Nilson-Weaver Typology (Chapter One) is a highly useful framework. Recall that their typology grows from the many ways in which Clemson faculty are currently using computer-enhanced learning. Let me rephrase their excellent list by citing the leading questions that a professor pursuing redesign might ask:

- How can data collection on students be meaningfully incorporated into my course?
- How can the computer assist me in judging (and grading) student progress?
- How can I allow students to self-assess progress or otherwise learn about themselves?
- How about designing student research projects into my course?
- How can simulation be used to stimulate student interest and active learning?
- Where can I combine access to digitized information with interactive assessment and participation?
- How can I design the course to encourage students to help each other learn? Can teaming be meaningfully built into my course?
- What learning exercises can I work into my course?

The Brown Typology, derived from the work of 150 professors at forty-three universities, is equally useful. Here are questions that professors seeking redesign can meaningfully ask, following in the footsteps of their computing-enhancing predecessors; some of them overlap with those I derived from the Nilson-Weaver Typology, but others do not.

- How can I use the communication-enhancing capacities of the computer to increase student learning?
- How can we encourage students to help other students learn? How about team projects?
- Can I give student access to other professors? practitioners in the field? more advanced students? people with another point of view? a special mentor?
- How can I use the computer to build more controversy into my course? To highlight different ways of viewing the same issues?
- How can I give each student additional ways to learn the central material of the course?

Regarding this last point, can the professor diversify examples to match more closely the career aspirations of each student? Can he or she create an opportunity for students who wish to repeat a lecture or an exercise? Why not provide presentations of the central material in both textual and auditory and video form?

The experiences of other educators will rarely furnish an exact guide to what should be done by a professor, or be done with a different group of students, or in another discipline. They can, however, be a useful catalyst.

Future Possibilities

A laptop learning community is a living entity, always changing. Successes and failures, as well as new hardware and software and middleware, will continue to shape new possibilities. Most of all, the experiences of success and failure, of what works and what does not, advance the art of teaching and learning.

Each of us has a hunch about the future. Some trends are well established. Others are purely speculative. As catalyst for further thought and experimentation, I offer this short list of likely developments in the future.

- The digital materials on the market today are "first generation." Over the next decade, we can expect higher-quality materials to accumulate. We'll have a much better idea about what works and what doesn't. New exchanges and business arrangements will make economically feasible the investment necessary to create quality, interactive learning objects.
- Publications such as this volume will chronicle the pedagogical successes and failures. Extensive indexing will allow a professor to research the experiences of others who work in a similar technological environment, who teach similar subject matter, who instruct face-to-face or only in an online environment, and who manage both large classes and small. Entering quality materials into these monitored databases will often count toward promotion and tenure decisions.
- Almost all courses will be built around team projects; much as in business and industry today, peers will complement grading by expressing

their opinions about the usefulness of colleagues' contributions to the team outcome and their own learning.

• The current trend toward collaborative team learning will continue, and it will be supplemented by new protocols for assessing or certifying individual contributions and achievements.

• Teaching in most universities will proceed on the assumption that all students have continuous access to the Internet.

• The movement toward wireless campuses will expand toward creation of wireless communities—that is, broad geographic areas (such as an entire city) where wireless connectivity is taken for granted.

• In technologically more sophisticated environments, universal ownership of tablet laptop computers will enable students to time-coordinate the notes they take with the words and images projected by their professor. (Such programs are currently available, but not yet at a reasonable cost).

• Now at the dawn of subgrouping methodology, we can expect students to innovate new ways to form and sustain groups.

• Graduating students will stay in touch with classmates, maintain access to the resources being made available to subsequent generations of students, and use their laptops to keep current in their profession.

• Some disciplines will expect participants to exchange information prior to the annual meeting and use laptops during the meeting.

• Migration toward student-centered curricula, enabled by customized education, will continue.

• Cooperative learning will supplement competitive learning.

• Unstructured chat sessions will disappear as a component of courses.

• New feedback mechanisms will be built into most course management products (for example, Blackboard and WebCT).

• More and more course administration tasks will be transferred to the students, freeing professors to work at individualizing the learning experience.

• Chunks of materials will replace textbooks.

Thanks to Clemson

Thanks, Clemson. You have created the model. Hopefully, similar volumes will be produced by other universities, groups of disciplinary scholars, students, and training professionals. Your volume and those that will follow allow all of us to broaden our vision about the possibilities of course redesign. Through specific examples, you are exciting our imagination—and for some you are enlivening creative redesign. I expect that this will become the first of many volumes in which faculty share their teaching motives and methods.

DAVID G. BROWN *is provost emeritus and professor of economics emeritus at Wake Forest University.*

INDEX

Back Issue/Subscription Order Form

Copy or detach and send to:
Jossey-Bass, A Wiley Imprint, 989 Market Street, San Francisco CA 94103-1741

Call or fax toll-free: Phone 888-378-2537 6:30AM – 3PM PST; Fax 888-481-2665

Back Issues: Please send me the following issues at $27 each
(Important: please include ISBN number with your order.)

_____

_____

_____

$ _____ Total for single issues

$ _____ SHIPPING CHARGES: SURFACE   Domestic Canadian
                                   First Item $5.00 $6.00
                                   Each Add'l Item $3.00 $1.50
               For next-day and second-day delivery rates, call the number listed above.

Subscriptions Please __ start __ renew my subscription to *New Directions for Teaching and Learning* for the year 2___ at the following rate:

U.S.	__ Individual $80	__ Institutional $170
Canada	__ Individual $80	__ Institutional $210
All Others	__ Individual $104	__ Institutional $244

**For more information about online subscriptions visit
www.interscience.wiley.com**

$ _____ Total single issues and subscriptions (Add appropriate sales tax for your state for single issue orders. No sales tax for U.S. subscriptions. Canadian residents, add GST for subscriptions and single issues.)

__Payment enclosed (U.S. check or money order only)
__VISA __ MC __ AmEx #_____ Exp. Date _____

Signature _____ Day Phone _____
__ Bill Me (U.S. institutional orders only. Purchase order required.)

Purchase order # _____
Federal Tax ID13559302   **GST 89102 8052**

Name _____

Address _____

_____

Phone _____ E-mail _____

For more information about Jossey-Bass, visit our Web site at www.josseybass.com

electronic ratings of instruction. They identify the advantages, consider costs and benefits, explain their solutions, and provide recommendations on how to facilitate online ratings.
ISBN: 0-7879-7262-2

TL95   **Problem-Based Learning in the Information Age**
Dave S. Knowlton, David C. Sharp
Provides information about theories and practices associated with problem-based learning, a pedagogy that allows students to become more engaged in their own education by actively interpreting information. Today's professors are adopting problem-based learning across all disciplines to faciliate a broader, modern definition of what it means to learn. Authors provide practical experience about designing useful problems, creating conducive learning environments, facilitating students' activities, and assessing students' efforts at problem solving.
ISBN: 0-7879-7172-3

TL94   Technology: Taking the Distance out of Learning
Margit Misangyi Watts
This volume addresses the possibilities and challenges of computer technology in higher education. The contributors examine the pressures to use technology, the reasons not to, the benefits of it, the feeling of being a learner as well as a teacher, the role of distance education, and the place of computers in the modern world. Rather than discussing only specific successes or failures, this issue addresses computers as a new cultural symbol and begins meaningful conversations about technology in general and how it affects education in particular.
ISBN: 0-7879-6989-3

TL93   Valuing and Supporting Undergraduate Research
Joyce Kinkead
The authors gathered in this volume share a deep belief in the value of undergraduate research. Research helps students develop skills in problem solving, critical thinking, and communication, and undergraduate researchers' work can contribute to an institution's quest to further knowledge and help meet societal challenges. Chapters provide an overview of undergraduate research, explore programs at different types of institutions, and offer suggestions on how faculty members can find ways to work with undergraduate researchers.
ISBN: 0-7879-6907-9

TL92   The Importance of Physical Space in Creating Supportive Learning Environments
Nancy Van Note Chism, Deborah J. Bickford
The lack of extensive dialogue on the importance of learning spaces in higher education environments prompted the essays in this volume. Chapter authors look at the topic of learning spaces from a variety of perspectives, elaborating on the relationship between physical space and learning, arguing for an expanded notion of the concept of learning spaces and furnishings, talking about the context within which decision making for learning spaces takes place, and discussing promising approaches to the renovation of old learning spaces and the construction of new ones.
ISBN: 0-7879-6344-5

TL91 Assessment Strategies for the On-Line Class: From Theory to Practice
Rebecca S. Anderson, John F. Bauer, Bruce W. Speck
Addresses the kinds of questions that instructors need to ask themselves as
they begin to move at least part of their students' work to an on-line format.
Presents an initial overview of the need for evaluating students' on-line work
with the same care that instructors give to the work in hard-copy format.
Helps guide instructors who are considering using on-line learning in
conjunction with their regular classes, as well as those interested in going
totally on-line.
ISBN: 0-7879-6343-7

TL90 Scholarship in the Postmodern Era: New Venues, New Values, New
Visions
Kenneth J. Zahorski
A little over a decade ago, Ernest Boyer's *Scholarship Reconsidered* burst upon
the academic scene, igniting a robust national conversation that maintains
its vitality to this day. This volume aims at advancing that important
conversation. Its first section focuses on the new settings and circumstances
in which the act of scholarship is being played out; its second identifies and
explores the fresh set of values currently informing today's scholarly
practices; and its third looks to the future of scholarship, identifying trends,
causative factors, and potentialities that promise to shape scholars and their
scholarship in the new millennium.
ISBN: 0-7879-6293-7

TL89 Applying the Science of Learning to University Teaching and Beyond
Diane F. Halpern, Milton D. Hakel
Seeks to build on empirically validated learning activities to enhance what and
how much is learned and how well and how long it is remembered. Demonstrates that the movement for a real science of learning—the application of
scientific principles to the study of learning—has taken hold both under the
controlled conditions of the laboratory and in the messy real-world settings
where most of us go about the business of teaching and learning.
ISBN: 0-7879-5791-7

TL88 Fresh Approaches to the Evaluation of Teaching
Christopher Knapper, Patricia Cranton
Describes a number of alternative approaches, including interpretive and
critical evaluation, use of teaching portfolios and teaching awards,
performance indicators and learning outcomes, technology-mediated
evaluation systems, and the role of teacher accreditation and teaching
scholarship in instructional evaluation.
ISBN: 0-7879-5789-5

TL87 Techniques and Strategies for Interpreting Student Evaluations
Karron G. Lewis
Focuses on all phases of the student rating process—from data-gathering
methods to presentation of results. Topics include methods of encouraging
meaningful evaluations, mid-semester feedback, uses of quality teams and
focus groups, and creating questions that target individual faculty needs and
interest.
ISBN: 0-7879-5789-5

TL86   Scholarship Revisited: Perspectives on the Scholarship of Teaching
        Carolin Kreber
        Presents the outcomes of a Delphi Study conducted by an international
        panel of academics working in faculty evaluation scholarship and
        postsecondary teaching and learning. Identifies the important components of
        scholarship of teaching, defines its characteristics and outcomes, and
        explores its most pressing issues.
        ISBN: 0-7879-5447-0

TL85   Beyond Teaching to Mentoring
        Alice G. Reinarz, Eric R. White
        Offers guidelines to optimizing student learning through classroom activities
        as well as peer, faculty, and professional mentoring. Addresses mentoring
        techniques in technical training, undergraduate business, science, and liberal
        arts studies, health professions, international study, and interdisciplinary
        work.
        ISBN: 0-7879-5617-1

TL84   Principles of Effective Teaching in the Online Classroom
        Renée E. Weiss, Dave S. Knowlton, Bruce W. Speck
        Discusses structuring the online course, utilizing resources from the World
        Wide Web and using other electronic tools and technology to enhance
        classroom efficiency. Addresses challenges unique to the online classroom
        community, including successful communication strategies, performance
        evaluation, academic integrity, and accessibility for disabled students.
        ISBN: 0-7879-5615-5

TL83   Evaluating Teaching in Higher Education: A Vision for the Future
        Katherine E. Ryan
        Analyzes the strengths and weaknesses of current approaches to evaluating
        teaching and recommends practical strategies for improving current
        evaluation methods and developing new ones. Provides an overview of new
        techniques such as peer evaluations, portfolios, and student ratings of
        instructors and technologies.
        ISBN: 0-7879-5448-9

TL82   Teaching to Promote Intellectual and Personal Maturity: Incorporating
        Students' Worldviews and Identities into the Learning Process
        Marcia B. Baxter Magolda
        Explores cognitive and emotional dimensions that influence how individuals
        learn, and describes teaching practices for building on these to help students
        develop intellectually and personally. Examines how students' unique
        understanding of their individual experience, themselves, and the ways
        knowledge is constructed can mediate learning.
        ISBN: 0-7879-5446-2

DATE DUE

Enhancing learning with
laptops in the classroom